The Office: The Scripts, ...

The Office:

The Scripts, Series 2

Ricky Gervais and Stephen Merchant

BBC
BOOKS

Published by BBC Books, BBC Worldwide Limited, Woodlands, 80 Wood Lane, London W12 0TT

ISBN: 0 563 52153 8

First published 2003.

This edition produced for The Book People Ltd, Hall Wood Avenue, Haydock, St Helens WA11 9UL

Commissioning Editor: Ben Dunn. Project Editor: Sarah Lavelle.
Designers: Linda Blakemore and Bobby Birchall (DW Design). Production Controller: Kenneth McKay.

Set in Helvetica Neue
Printed and bound in Great Britain by Butler & Tanner Limited, Frome, Somerset.

Contents

WERNHAM HOGG N E W S

Written and Edited By David Brent

Issue no.
4

MONKEY BUSINESS

FOR those of you who remember Pete Gibbons, congrats are in order.

His lovely wife Jan is pregnant again! If the baby is anything like his dad, it'll probably be late!

This week's competition is – guess who the father is! Ha ha, only joking Pete.

GIBBO

For those who don't remember Gibbo, he was with us from 1989 to 2000, but took voluntary redundancy to deal with troubles in his marriage.

Let's hope this baby brings them closer together.

SWEPT AWAY

BEST wishes to cleaner Joan Reynolds. She's been a familiar face at Wernham Hogg since 1985 and retired last week.

PATHETIC

An enjoyable send-off at the Four Horseshoes was only marred by so few people turning up.

Six out of fifty-two staff members is frankly pathetic.

WASH OUT

Not only was Joan disappointed at the sheer amount of food wasted, but she was understandably tearful when she saw the accounts department playing pool in the Duke of York next door.

Their excuse was that they looked in and deemed it a "bit of a wash out".

Well guys and gals, perhaps if you had made up the numbers it wouldn't have been so dull!

KEITH'S MASSIVE

BIG up yourself! "Big' being the operative word. Amateur DJ Keith Bishop (Accounts Department, Slough) is hitting the 'big time'.

If the kind of dance music you like is hard house then it won't be hard for you to leave your house and head down to Chasers Nightclub next Tuesday. Keith will be there 'largin' it and 'bigging up' the Slough 'massive' aiiit!

Keith, who weighs 19 stone (hence the jokes) says it doesn't get in the way of his mixing. But just don't get stuck behind him if there is a fire evacuation! (Heaven forbid, fire is no laughing matter.)

BABES IN THE (PLANET HOLLY WOOD)

EVER wanted to travel in a stretch limo, dine with the stars in trendy Planet Hollywood and then watch T'Pau live in concert?

If the answer is yes, then you'll want to know that the party animals from credit management are organising another wild night in the big smoke.

Tickets are £50, but that includes everything. Organiser Sheila Martinez says: 'The faint hearted should not apply because it's always a crazy night. We went clubbing last year. I saw Sinbad from Brookside and Josh, one of the gays from Big Brother 2.'

TILE HITLER

A STICKER promoting the Anti-Nazi League has been stuck on to a wall in one of the gents' urinals.

Much as I agree with the sentiment (the Nazis caused untold suffering during the 30s and 40s and even today there are despicable groups who champion their prejudice) I have been informed by Gordon in maintenance that materials and labour to have it removed could cost up to £30.

Please remember: vandalism has rarely solved anything.

BRENT VENTS

Your editor's views on the news

WORLD leaders and scientists continue to search for a way to wipe out the drought that ravages many parts of the third world. The solution is simple; just tell them to leave their umbrellas at home. It's guaranteed to rain then!!!

APOLOGY

I've had several e-mails complaining about a suggestion I made in this column that we should give cannabis to anorexics so they get the munchies. This was a satirical joke and was not meant to offend. I do not advocate the use of illegal drugs and I do not find any eating disorders amusing.

David Brent
Editor

Paper View by Vince

"We've got the Bank of England Contract. It's a licence to print money!"

David Brent

From: David Brent
Sent:
To: All Staff
Subject:

I have just received a phone call from former cleaner Joan, who was in tears. She had read my last newsletter and felt that my article about her leaving do being a wash-out suggested she was an unpopular person. Can I please now state for the record that no one is to show Joan copies of the newsletter. She is no longer an employee and consequently does not have any right to know what current employees may or may not think of her.

David

David Brent

From: David Brent
Sent:
To: All Staff
Subject:

I have appeased Joan by sending her an expensive bunch of flowers and a dustpan and brush sprayed gold – a whimsical and affectionate gift relating to the fact that she was a cleaner all her life. She was delighted and we had a nice chat about the fact that she misses us all.

However, you still MUST NOT SHOW HER ANY INTERNAL CORRESPONDENCE.

I know there has recently been much upheaval and you have lost colleagues to redundancy and retirement.

Life goes on!

If we're being honest I find it hard to believe that any of the people who left were actual friends of anyone here. Yes, they were good workers but contributed nothing on a social level. For example, Malcolm was a nice enough bloke but boring.

I personally do not really miss any of them.

Let's hope the new Swindon intake is more fun.

David

David Brent

From: David Brent
Sent:
To: All Staff
Subject: My previous e-mail

To whoever is leaking information: please do not tell Malcolm I think he is boring.

David

David Brent

From: David Brent
Sent:
To: All Staff
Subject:

I have just had an informative chat on the phone with Neil Godwin, my counterpart down in Swindon. He's been filling me in on what to expect from the new intake and good news! One of them is a lovely lady called Brenda who is confined to a wheelchair. Please note: she is to be treated the same as everyone else. I am reliably informed that apart from her appearance she is totally normal and has all of her faculties (e.g. mind).

David

David Brent

From: David Brent
Sent:
To: All Staff Swindon
Subject: Hello Swindon!

Dear Neil et al. Just a quickie. (Ooh cr matron!) Looking forward to your imminent arrival. My team here are very excited about the forthcoming assimilation. I'm sure some of you are nervous and will be leaving behind friends and family but I'm certain that once you see what a relaxed, easy-going place we have here, Swindon will be a distant memory.

To Brenda – I have warned the guys here of your condition so that when they see you for the first time they will not be shocked. In fact they are all delighted. Let me reassure you that we are fully equipped to receive someone like yourself. Not only have we had a ramp installed but one of the girls in accounts does regular volunteer work with Down's syndrome people.

You're in good hands!

See you all next week,

David

Episode **One**

CAST
David Brent RICKY GERVAIS
Tim MARTIN FREEMAN
Gareth MACKENZIE CROOK
Dawn LUCY DAVIS
Neil PATRICK BALADI
Rachel STACEY ROCA

with
Jennifer STIRLING GALLACHER
Lee JOEL BECKETT
Brenda JULIE FERNANDEZ
Trudy RACHEL ISAAC
Keith EWEN MACINTOSH
Oliver HOWARD SADDLER

and
Ben Bradshaw, Jamie Deeks, Patrick Driver, Jane Lucas, Tony MacMurray, Emma Manton, Alexander Perkins and Philip Pickard

PRE-TITLES SEQUENCE. SCENE 1. INT. OPEN-PLAN OFFICE. DAY.

TIM IS SITTING AT HIS DESK. FOR THE FIRST EVER TIME, HE LOOKS AS THOUGH HE'S WORKING HARD. GARETH ENTERS.

TIM:
Morning Gareth.

GARETH SITS DOWN AND STARTS SINGING THAT INFURIATING *MUPPET SHOW* SONG: 'MAH-NA-MAH-NAH'. ANOTHER EMPLOYEE COMES OVER AND JOINS IN.

TIM TRIES HARD TO IGNORE THIS.

SUDDENLY DAVID BRENT APPEARS FROM HIS OFFICE, GRINNING WILDLY, AND JOINS IN WITH THE SONG.

THEY'RE NOW ALL SINGING AND BOPPING AROUND. THEY'RE HAVING THE TIME OF THEIR LIVES. TIM IS NOT.

EVENTUALLY THEY FINISH SINGING AND GO BACK TO WHAT THEY WERE DOING.

BRENT: (giggling)
Muppets ...

OPENING TITLES

TIM TALKING HEAD. INT. DAY.

TIM:
No, I'm not giving up the idea of going to university. It's not like I'm never going to go, it's just that I've been made Senior Sales Rep., which is a great opportunity for me. There's people now coming in from Swindon, which is a new and exciting sort of venture for me as well. I'm thirty, time to grow up, basically. It's that simple.

SCENE 2. INT. OPEN-PLAN OFFICE. DAY.

TIM AND GARETH ARE AT THEIR DESKS, WORKING. TIM IS ON THE PHONE DOING BUSINESS, BEING EFFICIENT AND SOUNDING RESPONSIBLE.

TIM:
Listen, I suggest we put this down as a lesson, right? You have this stuff over to me by three o'clock today ... Three o'clock today, please ... Alright, then we'll say 'no harm done'. Alright? Okay ... See ya.

GARETH TAKES A CALL ON HIS MOBILE.

GARETH:
Gareth Keenan. Who's that? Oggy! Oggy oggy oggy! Oink oink oink!

TIM REACTS.

GARETH:
Oggy oggy oggy, oink oink oink! Oggy – oggy – oggy oggy oggy! Oink oink oink! ... Yeah, I'll see you later.

HE HANGS UP.

TIM:
Do you still keep in touch with Oggy?

GARETH:
That was Oggy just then.

TIM:
Was it? How is he?

GARETH:
He's fine. You don't even know him.

TIM:
No, I wish I did, he sounds great.

GARETH:
He is actually.

TIM: (angry)
One thing Gareth: when you're on the phone, could you keep the pig impersonations down to a minimum?

GARETH:
Yeah. Here we go. I've told you before. You can't tell me what to do, I'm Team Leader.

TIM:
Well, actually Gareth, I'm Senior Sales Rep., so, yes I can.

GARETH:
Er, Team Leader beats Senior Sales Rep.

TIM:
No, no, no it doesn't. My job title actually means something Gareth, yeah? I've got a pay rise, I'm on a new scale. Team Leader doesn't mean anything, mate.

GARETH:
Excuse me, it means I'm leader of a team.

TIM:
No it doesn't, it's a title someone's given you to get you to do something they don't want to do for free, right? It's like making the div kid at school milk monitor. No-one respects it.

GARETH:
Er, I think they do.

TIM:
No, they don't, Gareth.

GARETH:
Er, yes they do, 'cos if people were rude to me then I used to give them their milk last so it was warm.

TIM REACTS.

SCENE 3. INT. OPEN-PLAN OFFICE. DAY.

SCENES OF OFFICE LIFE.

BRENT IS HOVERING AT HIS OFFICE DOORWAY. AN EMPLOYEE IS OUTSIDE, TRYING TO SEND A FAX. SUDDENLY BRENT COMES OUT AND COLLARS HIM.

BRENT:
Oh no, I was going through some old stuff. Found that. Do you remember that? 'Inside Paper'. It's the trade magazine for the paper industry. My ugly mug on the front. Oh no ... Embarrassing.

SILENCE. THE EMPLOYEE IS NOT INTERESTED AND HAS NOTHING TO SAY.

<u>BRENT:</u> (a bit annoyed)
Alright …

HE BRUSHES THE EMPLOYEE AWAY, AS IF TO SAY, 'IF YOU'RE NOT INTERESTED, SOD OFF.' BRENT IS LEFT, HAVING MADE A FUSS IN FRONT OF THE CAMERA. HE REALISES THIS IS FAINTLY EMBARRASSING AND MUTTERS TO HIMSELF TO TRY TO GET OUT OF IT.

<u>BRENT:</u>
He's put me off what I was doing now, where was I … ? Oh yeah, making those phone calls.

HE SIDLES BACK INTO HIS OFFICE.

<u>SCENE 4. INT. RECEPTION. DAY.</u>

DAWN IS BEHIND THE RECEPTION DESK CANOODLING WITH HER FIANCE LEE. TIM APPROACHES AND DROPS A PACKAGE INTO HER IN-TRAY.

<u>TIM:</u>
Hello Dawn. Someone's coming to collect that later, so if you could …

<u>DAWN:</u>
Okay …

TIM WALKS AWAY. HE DOUBLES BACK.

<u>TIM:</u> (to LEE)
I wouldn't get caught behind there today, mate, because there's new people coming in and top brass are milling about so you should, er …

<u>DAWN:</u>
It'll be fine.

<u>LEE:</u>
I'm going anyway, mate.

DAWN:
Bye.

LEE KISSES DAWN THEN WALKS AWAY. TIM WATCHES HIM GO.

TIM:
I'm sorry about that, it's just I've got to supervise everything and make sure it's all sort of, you know …

HE STARTS TO WALK AWAY.

DAWN:
You haven't visited for ages.

TIM:
Oh, yeah, well, I'm busier now, I'm sort of a bit snowed under, so …

DAWN:
But you're alright though?

TIM:
Yeah, yeah, I'm fine. You?

DAWN:
Mmm, you'd have laughed –

DAWN'S PHONE RINGS.

TIM: (cutting her story short)
Phone.

TIM WALKS BACK TO HIS DESK.
DAWN WATCHES HIM GO AS SHE TAKES THE CALL.

SCENE 5. INT. RECEPTION. DAY

A HANDSOME 30-YEAR-OLD MAN IS STANDING AT RECEPTION. BRENT APPROACHES HIM.

BRENT:
It's all go.

DAWN:
This is Neil.

BRENT: (shaking his hand)
Neil Godwin.

NEIL:
Hi.

BRENT: (to camera)
Neil is Jennifer's replacement. He's sort of overseeing –

NEIL: (to camera)
I'm David's boss.

BRENT: (to camera)
Yes, just a tiny, a little bit above me, and that's only because it's –

NEIL: (to camera)
I'm the UK Manager. I was sort of David's equivalent in Swindon, and doing the same kind of job as him. Obviously my branch closed and now my staff are coming here, so I'm essentially David's boss, looking after him –

BRENT:
Well ... "Looking after" is the wrong term to use because we're both ...
(TO NEIL)
Good to meet you, though.

NEIL:
We have met before.

BRENT:
Have we?

NEIL:
Yeah. Ipswich Conference.

BRENT:
Oh God. I was a "leetle beet drunk"!

NEIL:
For most of the week, as I remember.

BRENT: (excited to be thought of as a rock 'n' roller)
Oh, doesn't sound like me does it, Dawn? Anyway … Come into my boudoir. Ooh!

DAWN WATCHES THEM GO, A FORCED SMILE ON HER FACE.

BRENT:
Is Jennifer with you?

NEIL:
No, she's on her way apparently.

BRENT:
Oh, part-timer.

THEY REACH THE HAT-STAND, WHICH NOW HAS 'MONKEY' IMPALED ON IT. BRENT STOPS AND POINTS IT OUT.

BRENT:
Monkey! That's an example of the laughs we have here – for one …

BRENT TALKING HEAD. INT. DAY.

BRENT:
Sure, we're in potentially traumatic times, but they are exciting times … with the merger. And things moved fast. Only two weeks ago I was telling them at the party I'd decided to stay after all and you saw how relieved they were at that. But we've had a personnel change of twenty, twenty-five per cent, you know, people coming and going. Redundancies – some voluntary, some involuntary, which is always hard. I had to let my PA go – last in, first out – which, you know, was really sad. That was upsetting. I'm coping. I rolled with the punch, you know, and it turns out that Dawn can do a lot of it anyway, so …

SCENE 6. INT. BRENT'S OFFICE. DAY

NEIL SITS IN FRONT OF BRENT'S DESK. BRENT SITS BEHIND IT, TRYING TO LOOK LIKE THE MASTER OF HIS DOMAIN. NEIL STARTS TAKING SOME PAPERWORK OUT OF HIS BRIEFCASE.

NEIL:
I'm sure there's going to be plenty of time for this later, I just thought I'd give you some of this while I think of it ...

BRENT IS SUBTLY PUSHING THE TRADE MAGAZINE, *INSIDE PAPER*, TOWARDS NEIL. NEIL ABSENT-MINDEDLY MOVES IT ASIDE. BRENT LEANS FORWARD TO RETRIEVE IT.

BRENT:
Oh, er, is that in the way?

NEIL:
No, you're alright.

HE HOLDS UP THE TRADE MAG.

BRENT:
You can put something down there 'cos I'll move that. Oh God. Look at that. Stupid – get UK manager of the month in 'Inside Paper' and pull a daft face. Typical.

NEIL:
You look quite young there.

BRENT:
Yeah, photogenic. Sort of natural.

NEIL: (noticing the cover date)
And it's eighteen months old.

BRENT: (caught out)
Yeah, I've been meaning to throw that away. I got it out today to throw it away. Definitely.

HE PLACES IT GENTLY ON TOP OF THE BIN.

BRENT:
There. Just look at that. 'Inside Paper'. 'Inside the Paper Bin' now. Recycle that. It's a shame 'cos ...

SCENE 7. INT. OPEN-PLAN OFFICE. DAY.

GARETH AND TIM ARE WORKING. GARETH HAS A BISCUIT TIN ON HIS DESK SHAPED LIKE A COMICAL NEW YORK COP. HE LIFTS THE LID AND TAKES A BISCUIT. A ROBOTIC AMERICAN VOICE BOOMS OUT.

BISCUIT TIN:
Stop. Move away from the cookie jar!

TIM LOOKS UNIMPRESSED. GARETH SNIGGERS AND LIFTS THE LID AGAIN.

BISCUIT TIN:
Stop! Move away from the cookie jar!

BRENT SIDLES UP.

BRENT:
Hello.

GARETH:
Do you want a biscuit?

BRENT:
What is it?

BRENT LIFTS THE LID.

BISCUIT TIN:
Stop! Move away from the cookie jar!

BRENT AND GARETH BOTH LAUGH. TIM ROLLS HIS EYES.

BRENT:
It's good, innit? Oh, d'you know this little thing we're doing lunchtime? Just a welcoming do for the new Swindon lot. Just a meet-and-greet and I'll be doing a speech, so no heckling.

GARETH:
I got a joke you can use.

BRENT:
Well, you don't usually do jokes but go on …

GARETH:
Alright, it's Christmas dinner. Royal family, having their Christmas dinner. Camilla Parker-Bowles goes, "Okay, we'll play twenty questions. I'll think of something – you have to ask me questions and guess what it is." So what she's thinking is "a black man's cock".

BRENT:
Ooh, trust Camilla. Not racist is it?

GARETH:
No. So Prince Philip goes, "Is it bigger than the bread bin?" She goes, "Yes." Prince Charles goes, "Is it something I can put in my mouth?" She goes, "Yes." Queen goes, "Is it a black man's cock?"

BRENT:
Ha ha ha ha! She's guessed it from those clues.

GARETH:
Straight away.

BRENT:
Oh God, that's the sort of stuff I write but, I mean, you didn't write it – you just told it – but, you know … Well done. So, do it again.

BISCUIT TIN:
Stop! Move away from the cookie jar!

BRENT: (brandishing the notes for his speech)
Oh, look forward to this.

SCENE 8. INT. RECEPTION AREA. DAY.

THE NEW SWINDON INTAKE ARE ARRIVING AND ARE BEING GREETED BY THE SLOUGH REGULARS. GARETH IS TRANSFIXED BY BRENDA, A WOMAN IN A WHEELCHAIR. BRENT'S TALKING HEAD BEGINS OVER THIS.

BRENT TALKING HEAD. INT. DAY.

Big day today. The Swindon mob are arriving. I've laid on a little do for them, part of the job. If you're asking me what vibe I'm gonna lay down, it's going to be very much a just a chill-out, let's-get-to-know-each-other type of vibe.
(WE SEE THAT JENNIFER TAYLOR-CLARKE HAS ARRIVED AND IS TALKING TO BRENT AND NEIL.)
Jennifer's coming back just to oversee the transition. Very much holding Neil's hand – daunting for him, sure.

A GROUP OF EMPLOYEES ARE DEEP IN CONVERSATION. BRENT IS HOVERING BEHIND THEM, TRYING TO JOIN IN. DAWN HANDS HIM A GLASS OF WINE.

BRENT: (loudly towards new employees)
Oh no, Dawn … You know I don't drink!

THEY SLOWLY REACT TO THE INTERRUPTION.

BRENT:
Uh? Just … She gave me some wine and I went, "No, I don't drink".

SWINDON EMPLOYEE:
Do you not drink?

BRENT: (giggling and nudging Slough employee)
He says, "Do I not drink?"!

PAUSE.

SLOUGH EMPLOYEE: (resignedly)
Yeah, he drinks.

BRENT:
Just a little bit.

NO-ONE IS INTERESTED.

SCENE 9. INT. RECEPTION/MEETING ROOM. DAY

BRENT IS EXCITEDLY USHERING PEOPLE INTO THE MEETING ROOM.

BRENT:
Take a chair. Not literally! Ladies first. Oh, here we go.

NEIL:
Did you put the chairs out yourself?

BRENT:
Yes, it was worth the effort.

NEIL:
It's great.

BRENT:
Are you going to say a few words?

NEIL:
Just a few, nothing much.

BRENT:
Don't be nervous. Just keep it short and bring me on. Enjoy the show.

NEIL:
Okay.

BRENT GOES INTO THE ROOM, GIGGLING TO HIMSELF AT THE THOUGHT OF WHAT HE'S GOING TO SAY.

BRENT TALKING HEAD. INT. DAY.

BRENT:
Some people are intimidated when talking to large numbers of people in an entertaining way. Not me, you know, I have had experience. At one of the Coventry conferences, some of us put on a little revue. I was the main thing and I did impressions of the conference co-ordinator, Eric Hitchmough, and he talks like this and he always says this one thing. He says, "I don't agree with that in the workplace". And I did him as famous people. Like the compère would go, "Ladies and gentlemen, Lieutenant Columbo." And I'd come out in a mac and I'd go, "One final thing, my wife loves you, but I don't agree with that in the workplace!" That's great, and I did him as Basil Fawlty: "I think I mentioned it once but I got away with it and I don't agree with that in the workplace!" And they were cracking up, and he loved it, because there was nothing vicious, you know. Some comedians would have picked on other stuff, you know, been more nasty. Like, he's got a little withered hand like Jeremy Beadle – I didn't mention it. No need.

BRENT, NEIL AND JENNIFER ARE SITTING AT THE FRONT OF THE ROOM. NEIL GETS UP TO SPEAK.

NEIL:
Okay, hello everyone. For those of you that don't know me, my name's Neil Godwin. For those of you that do know me, keep schtum.

MILD LAUGHTER.

NEIL:
I'm a man of simple pleasures. I don't need lovely houses, beautiful girls and classy restaurants – so it's a good job I moved to Slough!

SOME LAUGHS AND A FEW "OOHS".

NEIL:
No, it's great to be in Slough, really it is – I've just spent a year in Beirut.

MORE LAUGHTER.

NEIL:
Now, I know David is feeling a bit worried about taking on all these new staff –

BRENT GETS TO HIS FEET BUT SHEEPISHLY HAS TO SIT DOWN AGAIN WHEN HE REALISES IT'S NOT YET HIS BIG MOMENT.

NEIL:
– because as manager it is going mean a lot more responsibility. He'll now have to delegate twice as much work!

LAUGHS AND CHEERING. BRENT SMILES, PLEASED TO BE PART OF THE JOKE.

NEIL:
But there will be perks for him – I'm sure he's looking forward to having a whole new group of men underneath him!

SOME GOOD-NATURED WHOOPING. BRENT LOOKS A LITTLE ANNOYED.

NEIL:
Anyway, here's the man at the top of the pile ... David Brent.

BRENT GETS UP. PEOPLE APPLAUD.

BRENT: (pointing to NEIL)
Wait! You know he was saying there about me being the top of the pile of men, like saying I'm gay, right? I'm not gay. In fact I can honestly say I've never "come over a little queer".

HE MIMES WANKING. THERE IS SOME NERVOUS MUTTERING.

<u>BRENT:</u>
Get to the real stuff, that's just … He put me off.

BRENT THUMBS THROUGH A THICK WAD OF HAND-WRITTEN NOTES.

<u>BRENT:</u>
Welcome to Slough, to the new people. My name's David Brent and I've always been in the paper industry, haven't I, yeah. My parents owned a paper shop – until it blew away. 'Cos it was paper.

THERE IS A FAINT RIPPLE OF GROANING. BRENT IS SLIGHTLY TAKEN ABACK BY THE LESS THAN OVERWHELMING RESPONSE.

<u>BRENT:</u>
There's better ones than that. Okay. Yeah. I'm not used to public squeaking, I piss-pronunciate a lot of my worms.

THERE IS NO RESPONSE. PEOPLE SIT STONY-FACED.

<u>BRENT:</u> (struggling)
Do you not – that's The Two Ronnies – do you not like that? That is classic stuff.

A MOBILE PHONE RINGS.

<u>BRENT:</u> (snapping)
Turn the phone off, that's part of it. If you're not concentrating you're not going to enjoy it as much …
(COMPOSING HIMSELF)
Focus. Okay. Anyway, good to have you all here from Swindon. 'Cos I hear they dropped an atomic bomb on Swindon. About fifteen quid's worth of damage.

THE AUDIENCE LOOKS STUNNED AND EMBARRASSED AT THIS MANGLED JOKE.

<u>BRENT:</u>
Right. Okay. Let's … Right. Oh, it's a good job Eric Hitchmough isn't here 'cos you know what he'd say: "I don't agree with that in the workplace!",

wouldn't he? Imagine if Eric was a Los Angeles detective – be a bit weird, wouldn't it?

(HE DOES HIS COLUMBO IMPRESSION)

"Yeah, one final thing, my wife loves you but I don't agree with that in the workplace!" What's that Eric, you've given up being a Los Angeles detective and you've started running a hotel in Torquay?

(HE LAUNCHES INTO HIS BASIL FAWLTY ROUTINE)

"Yes, don't mention the war, I mentioned it once but I think I got away with it. And I don't agree with that in the workplace!"

BRENT RESORTS TO BASIL FAWLTY'S GOOSE-STEPPING FUNNY WALK.

BRENT: (frustrated)
"I don't agree with that in the workplace!"

NO-ONE LAUGHS. HE IS DYING UP THERE.

BRENT:
Do you not know who Eric Hitchmough is?

PEOPLE SHAKE THEIR HEADS.

BRENT:
Who's been to the Coventry conference?

A COUPLE OF HANDS ARE RAISED.

BRENT:
Right, so do you not know Eric Hitchmough?

JAMIE:
Yeah, but I didn't know he talked like that.

BRENT:
He talks exactly like that, doesn't he Gareth?

GARETH:
I prefer that stuff you do about his little hand …

GARETH MIMES HIS LITTLE HAND.

BRENT:
I don't do stuff about his little hand.

GARETH:
Yeah, you do, the wanking claw …

BRENT: (to audience, desperate now)
Has everyone heard of Harry Enfield?

PEOPLE MURMUR SOFTLY.

BRENT: (confrontational)
Has everyone heard of Harry Enfield?

PEOPLE ANSWER "YES", SHOCKED BY THE AGGRESSION.

BRENT:
Yes, right then, okay. Then who's this? "I do not believe you wanted to do that. Only me."

THERE IS NO RESPONSE. BRENT IS CRUSHED.

BRENT:
Oh come on …
(ANGRY NOW)
Ahhh, you try something. And that's … Aah …

BRENT SITS BACK DOWN, A BROKEN MAN.

NEIL GETS UP AGAIN.

NEIL:
Erm, thanks David.

BRENT: (curt, hearing his name)
Uh?

NEIL:
Thanks.

BRENT: (ungracious)
Whatever, just …

NEIL:
Okay, there's plenty of wine and snacks left through there, so if you want to help yourselves to anything else, come through –

PEOPLE SHUFFLE OFF IN EMBARRASSED SILENCE. BRENT STAYS SEATED. EVERYONE AVOIDS LOOKING AT HIM AS THEY LEAVE.

SCENE 10. INT. RECEPTION AREA/OPEN-PLAN OFFICE. DAY.

A "WELCOME SWINDON" DRINKS PARTY IS IN PROGRESS. PEOPLE ARE MAKING STILTED SMALL TALK WHILE DRINKING CHEAP WINE FROM PLASTIC GLASSES.

GARETH IS TALKING TO BRENDA, THE WOMAN IN A WHEELCHAIR. HE DOESN'T REALLY KNOW WHAT TO SAY TO HER.

CUT TO: BIG KEITH LOOKING BORED.

CUT TO: TIM AND JENNIFER CHATTING. DAWN WALKS BY AND LOOKS HAPPY WHEN TIM CALLS HER OVER.

TIM:
Sorry, excuse me Jennifer. Dawn – sorry, I've just realised you've been off reception for an hour and I don't know if we're missing calls or what. Could you check? Could you check the messages?

DAWN NODS, A LITTLE TAKEN ABACK.

TIM:
Is that alright? Thanks very much mate. Cheers.

TIM RESUMES HIS CHAT WITH JENNIFER. DAWN WALKS AWAY, DISAPPOINTED ONCE AGAIN BY TIM'S CHANGE OF CHARACTER.

SCENE 11. INT. OPEN-PLAN OFFICE. DAY.

BRENT SIDLES UP NEXT TO A FEW OF THE SWINDON NEWCOMERS.

BRENT:
Hiya. Oh, lunchtime gigs. They're the worst, ain't they? I don't think Neil warmed you up, to be honest, that's why it went over their ...
(HE MIMES SOMETHING GOING OVER HIS HEAD)
He's not a professional comedian.

SWINDON EMPLOYEE #1:
He was funny though.

BRENT:
Yeah, but often an amateur will stitch up a professional.

THERE'S SOME AWKWARD SILENCE AND NODDING. IT'S THE FIRST TIME THESE PEOPLE HAVE SEEN A MAN QUITE LIKE THIS.

BRENT:
Here's one I should have told you, right ... The royal family, yeah, Christmas day, had lunch, sitting down and Camilla goes, "Let's play a game." Right? "Let's play twenty questions." I'll think of something and you've got to guess what I'm thinking of", and what she's thinking of is a black man's cock. So Charles goes, "Is it bigger than a bread bin?" and she goes, "Yes." Philip goes, "Can I put it in my mouth?", she goes, "Yes." So the Queen goes –

AS HE BEGINS THE PUNCHLINE, OLIVER, THE NEW BLACK EMPLOYEE, JOINS THE GROUP.

BRENT:
– "Is it a black m-"
(DRYING UP AS HE SEES OLIVER)
Hiya ...

OLIVER:
Sorry, were you telling a joke?

BRENT:
No, that was it.

<u>SWINDON EMPLOYEE #1:</u>
What did the Queen say?

<u>OLIVER:</u>
Come on then. What was the joke?

<u>SWINDON EMPLOYEE #1:</u>
It was about the royal family playing twenty questions.

<u>OLIVER:</u>
It's not the black man's cock one, is it?

<u>BRENT:</u>
Er … It might be. But bad, isn't it?

<u>OLIVER:</u>
No, it's alright, it's funny.

<u>BRENT:</u>
Harmless.
(PATRONISING OLIVER FOR "TAKING IT SO WELL")
Well done …

BRENT TURNS, LOOKING FOR SOME WAY TO SHIFT THE CONVERSATION ONTO SOMETHING ELSE. HE FINDS THE ANSWER OPPOSITE HIM IN THE FORM OF BRENDA IN HER WHEELCHAIR.

<u>BRENT:</u>
Have you all met the, er … this little lady … this lady … ?

<u>SCENE 12. INT. BRENT'S OFFICE. DAY.</u>

BRENT AND GARETH ARE SITTING NEXT TO EACH OTHER. JENNIFER AND NEIL ARE OPPOSITE THEM.

<u>JENNIFER:</u>
Well, it's a shame this had to happen on Neil's first day, but, well, I've just had a complaint from one of the new intake.

<u>BRENT:</u>
What complaint?

<u>JENNIFER:</u>
I can't believe that you think the way to welcome people is by telling racist jokes.

<u>BRENT:</u>
Wrong. No way. He'd heard it before, right? He thought it was funny, so I don't know why he's complaining now.

<u>JENNIFER:</u>
He? It was a woman.

<u>BRENT:</u>
Oh, I assumed it was the …
(HE SWIPES HIS HAND ACROSS HIS FACE AS THOUGH THAT MIGHT SUGGEST 'BLACKNESS', BUT THEN THINKS BETTER OF IT)
… the new guy. Whoever it was is wrong, because it isn't racist.

<u>JENNIFER:</u>
What is it?

<u>BRENT:</u>
What? The joke?

<u>JENNIFER:</u>
The gist of it.

<u>BRENT:</u>
It won't be funny now, will it?

<u>JENNIFER:</u>
I don't care, what's the content?

<u>BRENT:</u>
Royal family sitting at home Christmas day and Camilla goes, "Oh, let's play a game. I'll think of something and you have to guess what I'm thinking of", and what she's actually thinking of is "a black man's cock".

BRENT AND GARETH GIGGLE TOGETHER, ENJOYING THE JOKE.

BRENT:
So Charles goes, "Is it bigger than a bread bin?" Camilla goes, "Yes." So Philip goes, "Can I put it in my mouth?" Camilla goes, "Yes." So the Queen goes, "Oh, is it a black man's cock?"

GARETH LAUGHS.

BRENT: (pleased, pointing at GARETH)
And he's heard it before. So that's the sort of …

JENNIFER:
I can see why someone would find that offensive.

BRENT:
It's not racist though, is it? I didn't say anything bad about black people.

JENNIFER:
It's about a black man's cock.

BRENT:
Why is that racist? It just happens to be a black man's cock. It could equally –

JENNIFER:
– No, you're using the ethnic stereotype that all black men have large penises because you think that makes it funnier.

BRENT:
It's not an insult though, is it? It's a compliment if anything.

JENNIFER:
So what you're saying is that black people ought to be flattered that their only achievement in this world is having oversized genitalia?

BRENT:
I'm saying they shouldn't be ashamed of them.

JENNIFER:
It's a myth.

GARETH:
I don't know Jennifer, I could show you a magazine where literally –

HE HOLDS OUT HIS HANDS ABOUT A FOOT APART.

JENNIFER: (angered)
Could you?

GARETH:
Well, I haven't got it with me, but when are you next in?

BRENT:
I could change it. I could just say "big cock", not mention the colour.

JENNIFER:
Well, you could, or you could save those jokes for your free time and not tell them in the workplace.

BRENT: (childish, pointing to GARETH)
It was his joke, he told me it.

JENNIFER:
Whatever David, let's leave it there. You've heard my opinion on the matter, now shall we go back outside?

JENNIFER HEADS BACK TO THE PARTY. GARETH FOLLOWS HER. BRENT WALKS WITH NEIL.

BRENT: (to NEIL)
She's right to be careful, because some of them can be a little bit sensitive.

NEIL:
Sorry. Who can?

BRENT:
Some … people can take things the wrong way. Ooh! As an actor said to the bishop!

HE LAUGHS BUT SUDDENLY REALISES HE COULD BE IN TROUBLE AGAIN.

BRENT:
And that's not – a gay stereotype. I'm not saying that is the wrong way; I'm saying it's a way. Some women like it the wrong way, don't they, and they're straight. It doesn't matter if you're straight or gay, you know, a lot of people are – one in ten apparently – that seems a bit high, doesn't it? But, you know, if you – you might be gay, I mean …

(FLOUNDERING)

… if you are, good luck to you – just, just make sure it's legal and – be safe! Okay?

NEIL NODS, SLIGHTLY PUZZLED. THEY RE-JOIN THE PARTY.

GARETH TALKING HEAD. INT. DAY.

GARETH:
That's it, see. A lot of people can't keep up with what words are acceptable these days and what words aren't. It's like my dad, for example, he's not as cosmopolitan or as educated as me, and it can be embarrassing, you know? He doesn't understand all the new trendy words, like, he'll say "poofs" instead of "gays", "birds" instead of "women", "darkies" instead of "coloureds" …

SCENE 13. INT. OPEN-PLAN OFFICE. DAY.

PEOPLE ARE STANDING CHATTING. GARETH HAS HIS EYE ON RACHEL, THE YOUNGEST, MOST ATTRACTIVE NEW GIRL.

TIM IS HELPING HIMSELF TO THE SANDWICHES AND SNACKS THAT ARE LAID OUT ON A TABLE. UNSURPRISINGLY, BIG KEITH IS ALSO THERE, CHOWING DOWN.

KEITH:
Alright, Tim?

TIM:
Yes thanks, Keith.

RACHEL IS ALSO GETTING SNACKS. TIM BUMPS INTO HER.

RACHEL: (to TIM)
Hiya.

TIM:
Sorry, didn't mean to ... Do you know you've got a T-shirt with "Pot My Pink" on it?

RACHEL:
Do you play snooker?

TIM:
So, it's ... Rachel?

RACHEL:
Tim?

TIM:
Well done.

GARETH APPEARS FROM NOWHERE, WORRIED THAT HE'S MISSING OUT ON THE 'NEW TOTTY'.

GARETH:
Gareth Keenan. Gareth Keenan.

RACHEL:
Hiya.

KEITH: (out of nowhere)
Keith.

SCENE 14. INT. OPEN-PLAN OFFICE. DAY.

BRENT WALKS OVER TO JENNIFER, WHO IS TALKING TO A FEW PEOPLE, INCLUDING OLIVER.

BRENT:
Hey Jenny, so you've met Oliver?

<u>JENNIFER:</u>
Yes.

<u>BRENT:</u>
Yeah. Good lad.
(TO OLIVER)
We were having a laugh earlier, weren't we?

<u>OLIVER:</u>
Er ... Oh yeah.

<u>BRENT:</u>
Did you like that joke I told about the Royal Family?

<u>OLIVER:</u> (slightly puzzled)
Uh, yeah, yeah, it was funny.

<u>BRENT:</u> (feigning surprise)
Oh. Yeah.

<u>JENNIFER:</u>
David, we've talked about this and I think I've made myself perfectly clear.

<u>BRENT:</u>
Yep, interesting –

<u>JENNIFER:</u>
I'll see you later, David. Goodbye.

SHE WANDERS OFF.

<u>BRENT:</u> (to OLIVER)
She should chill out a bit more, shouldn't she? Maybe have a bit of the old ganja.

BRENT MIMES TAKING A DRAG ON A JOINT.

<u>BRENT:</u>
D'you know what I mean?
(HE GESTURES AT OLIVER)
'Course you do. Oh ... Meetings would be different, wouldn't they? "Yes, David, I've called this meeting because I want you to go down the twenty-four-hour garage and get me some Hob-Nobs". Munchies ... Like Scooby Doo. All

those Scooby Snacks. That's 'cos he's got the munchies, innit? Not so much Scooby Doo, Dooby dooby-doo.

(HE DOES A SCOOBY DOO IMPRESSION)

Shaggy!

HE STARTS LAUGHING HEARTILY AT HIS OWN JOKE.

SCENE 15. INT. BRENT'S OFFICE. DAY.

YET AGAIN BRENT IS EXPLAINING HIMSELF TO JENNIFER AND NEIL.

BRENT: (desperate now)
I was not advocating the use of drugs! I was talking to someone on their level, because I can communicate with people from all walks of life.

SCENE 16. INT. OPEN-PLAN OFFICE. DAY.

TIM IS STILL TRYING TO MAKE SMALL TALK WITH RACHEL. GARETH HAS INVEIGLED HIS WAY INTO THE CONVERSATION. TIM IS HOLDING A POLYSTYRENE BOWL OF CRISPS AND OFFERS THEM TO RACHEL.

TIM:
Do you want one?

GARETH: (just wittering)
Snacks.

TIM: (searching for something to ask RACHEL)
So, when did you come up?

RACHEL:
Saturday.

GARETH: (still wittering)
Ahh, Saturday.

TIM:
Was it your mum or your boyfriend, or whatever, drove you?

<u>RACHEL:</u>
No, my brother came up with me.

<u>TIM:</u>
Okay. You got a lot of ties in Swindon or you starting again up here?

<u>RACHEL:</u>
I'll be going back weekends.

<u>TIM:</u>
Oh right. Okay.

<u>GARETH:</u>
Sorry, so have you got a boyfriend or not?

<u>RACHEL:</u> (chuckling)
Er no, I haven't. Erm, I think I left my drink, I'm just gonna …

<u>TIM:</u>
Okay, see you in a bit.

SHE WALKS OFF.

<u>GARETH:</u> (aside to TIM)
Tim, I know you don't mean to but you're sort of cramping my style a bit.

<u>TIM:</u>
What?

<u>GARETH:</u>
I mean I'm kind of planning to get off with her.

<u>TIM:</u>
Gareth. What if I liked her?

<u>GARETH:</u>
I saw her first, mate.

<u>TIM:</u>
And how does that work?

GARETH POINTS AT HIS EYES AND THEN TOWARDS RACHEL.

TIM:
So? You've won that argument doing that, have you? Yeah, of course. That's won the argument.

SCENE 17. INT. RECEPTION. DAY.

PEOPLE ARE RETURNING TO THEIR DESKS.

TIM IS WALKING PAST RECEPTION. DAWN CALLS TO HIM.

DAWN:
Hi!

TIM:
Hi.

DAWN:
They came for the package.

TIM:
Oh they came, did they?

DAWN:
Yeah. No problem.

TIM:
Cool.

DAWN:
I'm so bored.

TIM:
Are you? Right. Okay.

DAWN:
Do you want to wind up Gareth for a bit?

TIM:
No. I don't think we should. He's a bit busy.

DAWN:
So?

TIM:
So am I Dawn, actually. So should you be …

DAWN LOOKS SHOCKED. TIM NEVER USED TO SPEAK TO HER LIKE THIS.

SCENE 18. INT. RECEPTION/OPEN-PLAN OFFICE. DAY.

PEOPLE ARE BACK AT WORK.

CUT TO: BRENT IN HIS OFFICE, STARING INTO SPACE, LOST IN THOUGHT.

CUT TO: DAWN LEANING ON HER RECEPTION DESK WATCHING TIM. TIM LOOKS ROUND AND SHE BREAKS HER GAZE, PRETENDING TO BE BUSY WORKING. TIM WALKS UP TO HER DESK.

TIM:
Dawn, hello. Listen, I've been checking my diary: I've been overlooking something – so have you actually – there's a twenty-minute window I've got here, it says to "wind up Gareth with Dawn".

DAWN BREAKS INTO A SMILE, RELIEVED AND EXCITED.

TIM:
So shall we do that, shall we? This way please, madam.

DAWN FOLLOWS TIM INTO THE MEETING ROOM. WE HEAR GARETH'S VOICE FROM INSIDE.

GARETH: (off-screen)
Oh no, please, I'm not in the mood. I'm working …

TIM: (off-screen)
Gareth, Gareth, just a quick one. Did you see that film last night? Gaylords Say No?

GARETH: (off-screen)
No …

WE HEAR DAWN LAUGHING.

CUT TO: BRENT STILL IN HIS OFFICE, LOST IN THOUGHT.

SCENE 19. INT. OPEN-PLAN OFFICE. DAY.

PEOPLE ARE WORKING. BRENT SUDDENLY APPEARS.

BRENT:
Sorry. Can I have a – hello – can I have a quick word with everyone? I'm mainly talking to the Swindon lot here. Some of you seem to have got off on the wrong foot with me, yeah? I don't think, you know, you didn't like some of the jokes I told earlier … You've got to chill out, yeah? Trust me. This is what I do. Alright? You will never work in a place like this again. This is brilliant – fact! Yeah? And you'll never have another boss like me, someone who's basically a chilled-out entertainer, yeah? Now, some of you maybe didn't understand the jokes I was making and misinterpreted one, and went to Jennifer, okay. Little bit annoyed that you thought you could go to Jennifer and not me. Who was it that complained? And it's not a witchhunt, just, who was it that … ?

TRUDY AND BRENDA FROM SWINDON PUT THEIR HANDS UP.

BRENT:
Okay, two of you, good. Right, you – why did you think you could go to Jennifer but not me?

TRUDY:
Because I don't know you, and I didn't like the kind of joke you were telling.

<u>BRENT:</u>
Well …

<u>TRUDY:</u>
And I don't think someone in your position should be laughing at black people.

<u>BRENT:</u>
It's funny that only two of you thought that out of everyone, but, you know …

<u>MALE SWINDON EMPLOYEE:</u>
Erm, I didn't like it either.

<u>BRENT:</u>
Right, proves my point. Swindon, you're new, you don't know me.

<u>SLOUGH EMPLOYEE:</u>
I'm not new and I found it quite offensive.

<u>BRENT:</u> (angry, pointing at OLIVER)
Right, well, he didn't, so …

<u>BRENDA:</u>
But what's he got to do with it?

<u>BRENT:</u>
Well, if he doesn't mind us laughing at him, what harm's been done is what …

<u>TRUDY:</u>
But why is it that only black people should be offended by racism?

<u>BRENT:</u>
Good point, yeah. First sensible thing you've said all day. Because I say come one, come all, we're all the same, yeah? Let's –

<u>TRUDY:</u>
So is that why you've only got one black guy in the whole organisation?

<u>BRENT:</u> (smug)
Wrong. Indian fella in the warehouse, and there used to be one Indian fella used to work up here – lovely chap – he left, he didn't like it. Up to him, you know. If I had my way, the place would be full of 'em –

HE POINTS TO OLIVER TO ILLUSTRATE WHO HE MEANS BY "THEM".

BRENT:
– wouldn't it, Gareth?

GARETH:
Yeah. Or half and half.

BRENT: (to OLIVER)
Yeah. You are half and half, aren't you?

OLIVER:
I'm mixed race, yes.

BRENT:
That is my favourite, yeah, that is what I'm trying to achieve ... That's the ...

(HE WEAVES HIS FINGERS TOGETHER)

... melting pot ... please?

(TO ROOM, POINTING AT HIMSELF)

So there's your racist for you!

BRENT IS THINKING "MY WORK HERE IS DONE" AND HE WALKS OFF INTO HIS OFFICE. PEOPLE GO BACK TO WORK, STUNNED.

TIM AND DAWN ARE LAUGHING TOGETHER ABOUT BRENT'S SPEECH. HE STARTS DANCING WITH HER AND SINGING.

TIM:
What the world needs is a great big melting pot ...

FROM NOWHERE, LEE APPEARS AND VIOLENTLY PUSHES TIM AGAINST THE WALL, SHOCKING EVERYONE WITH HIS FEROCITY. LEE STORMS OFF AND DAWN RUSHES AFTER HIM.

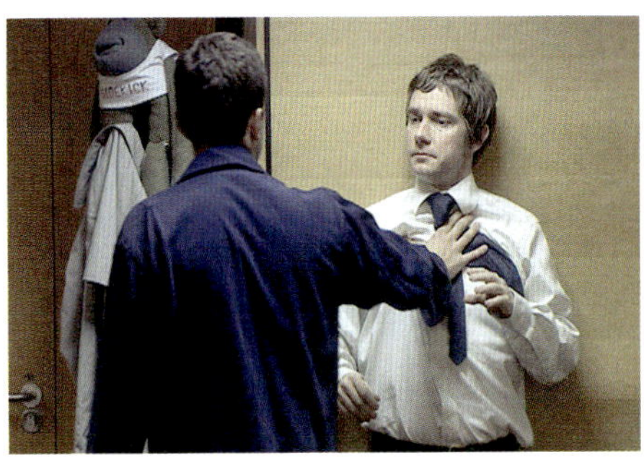

TIM IS LEFT TO STEW IN THE PAINFUL SILENCE. HE FEIGNS AN UNCONCERNED LAUGH AND SITS BACK DOWN AT HIS DESK.

CLOSING MUSIC AND END CREDITS, THEN:

DAWN IS TIDYING UP THE REMAINS OF THE BUFFET, ALONE.

Episode **Two**

CAST
David Brent RICKY GERVAIS
Tim MARTIN FREEMAN
Gareth MACKENZIE CROOK
Dawn LUCY DAVIS
Neil PATRICK BALADI
Rachel STACEY ROCA

with
Lee JOEL BECKETT
Brenda JULIE FERNANDEZ
Trudy RACHEL ISAAC
Keith EWEN MACINTOSH
Oliver HOWARD SADDLER

and
Ben Bradshaw, Jamie Deeks, Patrick Driver, Jane Lucas, Tony MacMurray, Emma Manton, Alexander Perkins and Philip Pickard

SCENE 1. INT. OPEN-PLAN OFFICE. DAY.

OFFICE SCENES.

BRENT SIDLES UP TO OLIVER'S DESK.

BRENT:
Hello. You alright?

OLIVER:
Yeah, good, thanks.

BRENT:
Did you see that film last night, it was Denzel Washington?

OLIVER:
No –

BRENT:
He's brilliant, he's a brilliant actor.

OLIVER:
He's very good, very good.

BRENT:
Oh dear …

OLIVER:
I like him.

BRENT:
He's great. Oh. See you later.

OLIVER:
Yeah, see you later.

BRENT STROLLS OFF. OLIVER RETURNS TO WORK.

PAUSE.

BRENT QUICKLY SIDLES BACK INTO VIEW.

BRENT:
He's not my favourite actor of all time, by the way.

OLIVER:
Oh no?

BRENT:
No. My favourite actor of all time is Mr Sidney Poitier.

OLIVER:
Oh ...

BRENT:
So. That's ... alright?

OLIVER:
Yes. Amazing.

OLIVER TRIES TO DIGEST WHAT HAS JUST HAPPENED.

SCENE 2. INT. DESK AREA. DAY.

GARETH IS SITTING USING A HAND-EXERCISER.

TIM:
Gareth, what, are you building up your wrists?

GARETH:
Yes.

TIM:
When is the charity wankathon?

GARETH:
I don't know, but you'd win it.

HE SMIRKS AT HIS OWN LIGHTNING WIT.

TIM:
That's good. Good. No, seriously, what are you doing?

__GARETH:__
Orienteering, aren't I, with the TAs ...

DAWN WALKS OVER, ACCOMPANIED BY LEE.

__TIM:__ (a little on edge)
Alright.

__LEE:__
Er, yeah. I just came to apologise for –

__TIM:__
Oh Lee, don't worry about it.

__LEE:__
No, no, no, I was out of order. I'd had a bad day, I was really wound up, so I shouldn't have done –

LEE PUTS A BOTTLE-SHAPED GIFT ON TIM'S DESK.

__TIM:__
No, I understand.

__LEE:__
So we're cool, yeah?

__TIM:__
Oh yeah. Absolutely. Yeah, totally cool.
(POINTING TO THE GIFT.)
What's that? Is that for me?

__LEE:__
Yeah.

__TIM:__
Oh, cheers. Thanks.

__GARETH:__
Just to put your mind at rest, there's nothing going on between them. 'Cos I would know: I've been watching him like a hawk. And I imagine you've been watching her your end, so between us we got it covered.

THEY ALL STARE AT GARETH AND THEN CHOOSE TO IGNORE WHAT HE'S JUST SAID.

LEE:
See you later, mate.

TIM:
Yeah. Alright. Thanks for that, mate. Cheers.

LEE AND DAWN WALK AWAY.

GARETH EYES THE BOTTLE-SHAPED GIFT.

GARETH:
Probably a bottle of something.

TIM:
You reckon?

GARETH:
Look at the shape.

SCENE 3. INT. BRENT'S OFFICE. DAY.

BRENT IS TALKING TO THE CAMERA. GARETH IS SITTING ON THE OTHER SIDE OF THE DESK, NODDING IN AGREEMENT.

BRENT:
Today I'm doing our staff appraisals, and some people can get a little bit nervous about that because they think they're walking the long mile to put their head on the block, which is wrong. They fill out a form in advance –

GARETH HOLDS ONE UP.

BRENT:
– and they don't only list their strengths and weaknesses, but also mine as a boss, you know? So it's a chance for them to tell me where we're going wrong, and we can … It's very much an opportunity to –

GARETH:
– to separate the wheat from the chaff!

BRENT:
Well, no, that sounds bad, this, you know, it's not a witch hunt. We're not trying to find out who the worst people are –

GARETH:
– well, we know who they are already.

BRENT:
Well, no –

GARETH:
I've written them on my form.

BRENT:
You shouldn't have written them on your form.

GARETH:
I've underlined the worst ones.

BRENT:
Well, you're missing the point.

BRENT GLANCES AT THE LIST, AND HE NODS IN AGREEMENT.

SCENE 4. INT. BRENT'S OFFICE. DAY.

TIM COMES IN FOR HIS APPRAISAL.

TIM:
Hello David.

BRENT:
Here he is.
(PLAYING TO CAMERA)
Tim Canterbury. Good man. The Canterbury Tales … by Chaucer.

TIM:
Yeah.

BRENT:
And Shakespeare … Pleased with you, very proud.

TIM:
Thank you.

BRENT:
New leaf, et cetera. Trust. Encouragement. Reward. Loyalty. Satisfaction.

HE ACCOMPANIES HIS WORDS OF WISDOM WITH SOME ILLUSTRATIVE HAND MOVEMENTS.

BRENT:
That's what I'm … Probably wondering why I am so generous with encouragement?
(POMPOUS)
"Trust people and they will be true to you; treat them greatly and they will show themselves to be great."

TIM LOOKS BAFFLED.

BRENT:
So, happier now? No looking back.

TIM:
Well, I am still eventually gonna go back to uni and do a psychology degree, but yeah –

<u>BRENT:</u>
No point, no point, no point. No point. Sure: Eighteen, nineteen, go to university, get it out of your system, you know. Waste time mucking around, getting drunk, getting up at midday –

<u>TIM:</u>
– having casual sex.

<u>BRENT:</u>
Having casual sex, you know, but we're in our thirties now.

<u>TIM:</u>
Well, I'm only just thirty. Are you, you must be thirty-nine?

<u>BRENT:</u> (dodging question)
No … Both in our thirties is the fact. Yeah? You know, who's to say, you keep your head down, in a few years' time you could be in the hot seat. Like me, so …

<u>TIM:</u> (musing)
When I'm nearly forty?

<u>BRENT:</u> (annoyed at the suggestion he's nearly forty)
Well, we're both in our thirties at the moment, is what I'm, you know … Just chewing the fat, but … Good, you're on the right lines.

ANOTHER EPIGRAM STRIKES HIM.

<u>BRENT:</u>
Can I just … "If we're facing in the right direction, all we have to do is keep on walking."

<u>TIM:</u>
Yeah. Very nice. You're quite a philosopher.

<u>BRENT:</u> (pleased)
Well, it's just that I think … "Our greatest glory is not in never falling, but in rising every time we fall."

<u>TIM:</u>
Are you reading these?

<u>BRENT:</u>
Am I what?

<u>TIM:</u>
Reading the quotes?

<u>BRENT:</u>
Sort of.

TIM LEANS OVER TO READ BRENT'S PIECE OF PAPER.

<u>TIM:</u> (reading)
Confucius, Bernard Shaw …

<u>BRENT:</u> (covering up the names)
It doesn't matter who said them first. I am passing on my wisdom to you.

<u>TIM:</u>
Cool.

<u>BRENT:</u> (pointing outside)
And don't tell those I've just been reading them.

<u>TIM:</u>
I'm not going to.

<u>BRENT:</u>
It's an insult. I'll put them down there if it's obvious.

HE HIDES THE PAPER ON THE FLOOR BENEATH HIS DESK.

<u>SCENE 5. INT. BRENT'S OFFICE. DAY.</u>

DAWN'S APPRAISAL IS UNDER WAY.

<u>DAWN:</u>
I always wanted to be a children's illustrator and when people said to me, "What do you do?", I would say, "Well, I'm an illustrator but I do some reception work for a bit of extra cash." And for years I was an illustrator who did some reception work. And then Lee thought it would be a good idea for us to both get full-time jobs. And, you know, then you're knackered after work and it's hard to fit in time for the illustrating. So now when people say, "What do you do?", I say, "I'm a receptionist."

<u>BRENT:</u> (missing the point because his mind has wandered)
And a bloody good one, and yeah, you'll always have the art, you know. Keep up the doodling, always, you know. Pipe dreams are good in a way.

<u>DAWN:</u>
Well, I still hope it will happen, to be honest.

<u>BRENT:</u>
Keep the dream alive because otherwise one day you'll go, "Oh, could I have made it?"

<u>DAWN:</u>
Yeah.

<u>BRENT:</u>
And if you keep trying, at least then when it doesn't happen, you can go, "At least I gave it a go", you know …

<u>SCENE 6. INT. SMOKERS' ROOM. DAY.</u>

TIM IS HAVING A COFFEE WITH RACHEL.

<u>TIM:</u>
Are you settling in alright?

RACHEL:
Yeah.

TIM:
Having fun?

RACHEL:
Er, yeah.

TIM:
Well, not fun, as much fun as you can have at Wernham Hogg. How long were you at Swindon?

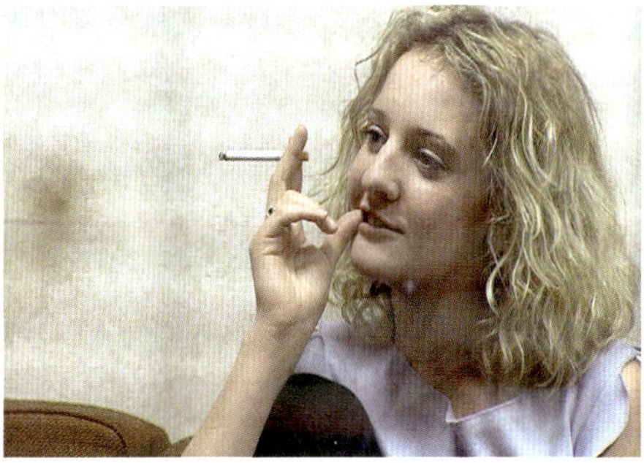

RACHEL:
Er, two years.

TIM:
Right.

RACHEL:
Two years.

TIM:
Right.

SCENE 7. INT. BRENT'S OFFICE. DAY.

BRENT IS STILL IN CONVERSATION WITH DAWN.

BRENT:
Okay, if you had to name a role model, someone who's influenced you, who would it be?

DAWN:
What, like a historical person?

BRENT:
No, someone in general life, just someone who's been an influence on you.

DAWN:
I suppose my mum. She's just strong, calm in the face of adversity. Oh God, I remember when she had her hysterectomy –

BRENT: (interrupting)_
– if it wasn't your mother though. I mean, it doesn't even have to be a woman, it could be a –

DAWN:
– a man?

BRENT:
Yeah.

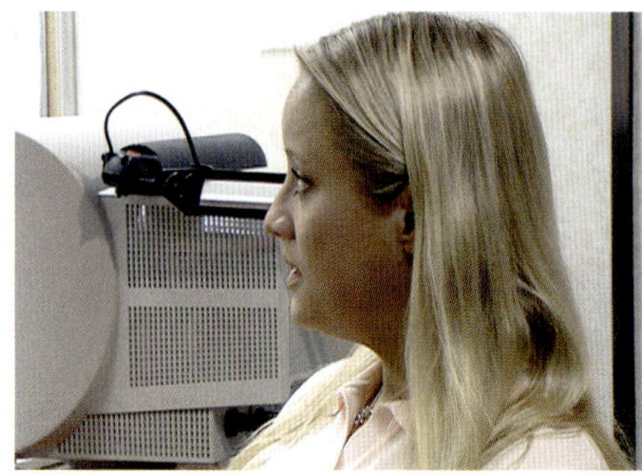

DAWN:
Okay, well I suppose if it was a man, it would be my father –

BRENT:
– not your father.

DAWN:
No?

BRENT:
Let's take your parents as read. I'm looking for someone in the, sort of, work-related arena whose influence –

DAWN:
Right. Okay. Well, I suppose Tim then, he's always –

BRENT:
– well, he's a friend, isn't he? Not a friend. Someone in authority. Maybe –

DAWN:
Well then, I suppose Jennifer –

BRENT: (annoyed)
I thought we said not a woman, didn't we, or am I –

DAWN:
Okay, well, I suppose you're the only one who –

BRENT: (mock-embarrassed)
Oh. Embarrassing. That's backfired, hasn't it? Oh dear. Very flattering, but can we put me, I don't know …

DAWN:
Okay, Tim then.

BRENT: (curt)
We said not Tim, so, do you wanna put me or not?

DAWN:
Okay.

BRENT:
Right. So shall I put "strong role model"?

DAWN:
Okay.

BRENT:
Yeah.

SCENE 8. INT. OPEN-PLAN OFFICE. DAY.

PEOPLE ARE WORKING. SUDDENLY A LOUD SIREN STARTS RINGING. IT'S THE FIRE ALARM.

BRENT EXITS HIS OFFICE.

BRENT:
Just a drill. Do not panic, okay?

GARETH RUSHES OVER AND STARTS USHERING PEOPLE OUT OF THE FIRE EXIT.

BRENT: (to camera)
Look, trained. Good man, you know.

GARETH:
Come on people, let's get moving. Do as you're told. Come on. Do not run and do not panic ...

HE CONTINUES SHOUTING INSTRUCTIONS.

BRENT: (to camera)
And I'd be the last one out in these situations, not because of my job description, that is what I'd do. I do these every couple of months, you know, you have to by law but that's not why I do them. It's because even though I'm always cool in a situation like this, some people are not, and so I try to make sure –

AS HE IS TALKING, BRENDA PASSES, BEING PUSHED IN HER WHEELCHAIR BY OLIVER. BRENT STOPS THEM.

BRENT:
I'll do that. It's alright.

PEOPLE TRY TO HELP.

BRENT:
No, no, no, no –

BRENT GRABS BRENDA'S WHEELCHAIR HANDLES. HE BENDS DOWN TO TALK TO BRENDA.

BRENT:
We're gonna get you out of here. Alright. So …

BRENT LOOKS AT THE CAMERA TO MAKE SURE EVERYONE HAS REGISTERED HIS CHARITY. HE PUSHES HER OUT OF THE ROOM.

SCENE 9. INT. STAIRWELL. DAY.

PEOPLE ARE MAKING THEIR WAY DOWN. TOGETHER, GARETH AND BRENT ARE CARRYING BRENDA, IN HER WHEELCHAIR, DOWN THE EMERGENCY STAIRS.

IT'S A STRUGGLE AND AS BRENT IS STILL TRYING TO TALK TO THE CAMERA, HE'S SOON OUT OF BREATH.

<u>BRENT:</u> (to camera)
Obviously – the lifts are out of bounds in a fire situation, so the important thing is –
(TO GARETH)
Put her down, will you?

OUT OF BREATH, THEY PUT THE WHEELCHAIR DOWN.

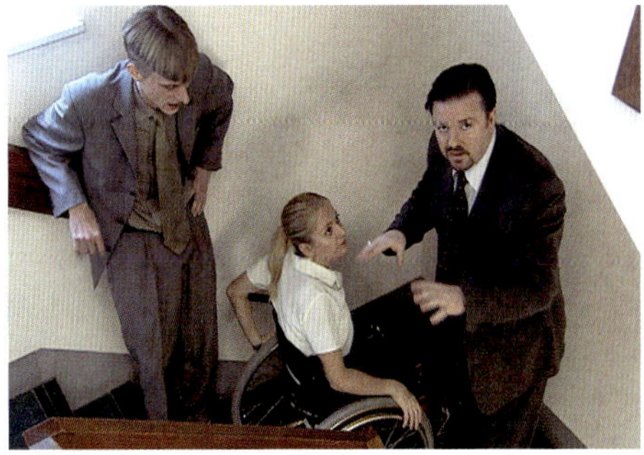

<u>BRENT:</u>
This isn't worth it. It's stupid … Obviously in a real situation we'd take her all the way down, but this is just a drill, so I think we can leave her here.

<u>BRENDA:</u>
Can't I just use the lift?

<u>GARETH:</u>
No. Not even in a drill. Never use the lift.

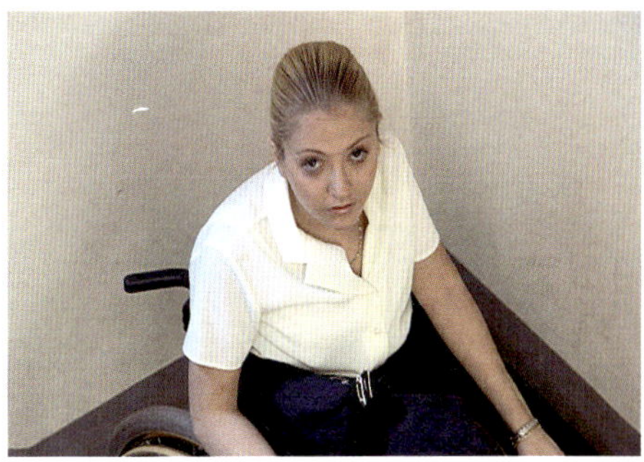

<u>BRENT:</u>
We'll be out … We'll be one minute, then we'll be back.

BRENT WALKS DOWN THE STAIRS HUFFING AND PUFFING. BRENDA, 'LEFT TO BURN', LOOKS FORLORNLY AT THE CAMERA.

<u>SCENE 10. EXT. CAR PARK. DAY.</u>

PEOPLE ARE GATHERED OUTSIDE. TIM IS PUTTING ON THE CHARM FOR RACHEL. DAWN REGISTERS THIS.

GARETH TALKING HEAD. INT. DAY.

GARETH:
I don't know if you're aware of the situation that's arising here. I usually stay clear of the ladies at work, but there is someone I've got my eye on. I won't say who, and I don't know what Tim's playing at, moving in. He's already embarrassed himself once before asking Dawn out, so this is only going to end in tears. Whereas I, you probably notice, play it cool. He's not a man of the world like me. I can read women and you've got to know their wants and their needs, and that can be anything from making sure she's got enough money to buy groceries each week to making sure she's gratified sexually after intercourse.

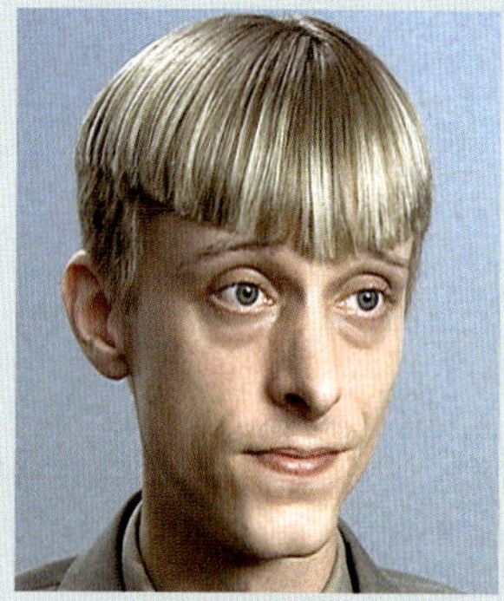

SCENE 11. EXT. CAR PARK. DAY

PEOPLE ARE STILL MILLING AROUND.

CUT TO: BRENDA STILL LEFT ABANDONED IN THE STAIRWELL.

IN THE CAR PARK, THE ALARM HAS STOPPED AND PEOPLE ARE MAKING THEIR WAY BACK INTO THE BUILDING. DAWN CATCHES UP WITH TIM ON THE WAY IN.

DAWN: (clearly jealous)
Noticed you were using all your best lines on Rachel.

TIM:
Best lines? Just being friendly.

DAWN:
Yes. Friendly. Sort of … more than …

TIM:
More than?

DAWN:
Friendly.

SCENE 12. INT. BRENT'S OFFICE. DAY.

BRENT IS GIVING BIG KEITH HIS APPRAISAL. IT'S SLOW GOING.

BRENT: (reading KEITH's form)
Under strengths, you've just put 'accounts'.

KEITH:
Yep.

BRENT:
That's your job, though, that's just …

KEITH:
Mmm.

BRENT:
No, Keith, I was sort of looking for your skills within your job so is there anything else you could've put there?

KEITH SHRUGS.

BRENT:
No? Okay, under weaknesses – you've put eczema …

SCENE 13. INT. SMOKERS' ROOM. DAY.

RACHEL IS CHATTING WITH DAWN.

DAWN:
You had a really fantastically welcoming buffet.

RACHEL:
The wine was something else …

DAWN:
And everyone's quite friendly

RACHEL:
Yeah, everyone's … And Tim … Tim seems nice.

DAWN:
Yeah.

RACHEL:
He's a good laugh. I was just gonna … Has he got a, a girlfriend, or – ?

DAWN: (laughing)
Tim? No.

RACHEL:
Why? What's up with him?

DAWN:
Oh, nothing. Why?

RACHEL:
Would you?

DAWN: (holding up her engagement ring)
Out of the equation.

RACHEL:
Yeah, I know, but if you weren't, would he be … ?

DAWN: (laughing nervously)
If I weren't … Madness.

SCENE 14. INT. BRENT'S OFFICE. DAY.

BRENT LOOKS THROUGH KEITH'S FORM.

BRENT:
Right, you've left this section completely blank, Keith. You haven't done the Q and A.

KEITH:
I thought that you filled that in.

BRENT:
No, no, no, no, this is aimed at you, look: "To what extent do you believe that you have the skills and knowledge to perform your job effectively?" And then you just tick one of the boxes. "Not at all." "To some extent." "Very much so." "Don't know." What would you tick?

KEITH:
Don't know.

BRENT:
Okay.
(HE TICKS THE BOX)
Question 2: "Do you feel you have received adequate training to use your computer effectively?"

KEITH:
What are the options?

BRENT: (slightly frustrated, but wanting to be encouraging)
Same as … They're always the same, always the same. "Not at all." "To some extent." "Very much so." "Don't know."

KEITH:
Don't know.

<u>BRENT:</u>
"Don't know" again? Okay. "Do you feel you are given the flexibility to decide how best to accomplish your goals?"

KEITH CHEWS GUM AND STARES BLANKLY AT BRENT.

<u>BRENT:</u>
Do you want the options again?

<u>KEITH:</u>
Yes.

<u>BRENT:</u>
"Not at all." "To some extent." Always the same. "Very much so." "Don't – "

<u>KEITH:</u> (interrupting)
Don't know.

<u>BRENT:</u> (slightly agitated)
If "Don't know" wasn't there, what would you put?

<u>KEITH:</u>
What are the options?

<u>BRENT:</u> (anger rising)
"Not at all." "To some extent." "Very much so." "Don't know."

<u>KEITH:</u>
Very much so.

<u>BRENT:</u>
Do you remember what the question was?

<u>KEITH:</u>
No.

<u>BRENT:</u>
Okay, do you … Let's … We're going to leave that there.

SCENE 15. INT. OPEN-PLAN OFFICE/MEETING ROOM. DAY.

THE CAMERA IS FOLLOWING BRENT TOWARDS THE MEETING ROOM.

BRENT: (to camera)
Just gonna give the new Swindon lot a bit of a … not an appraisal as such but, you know …

A LAUGH GOES UP FROM INSIDE THE MEETING ROOM. BRENT ENTERS. THE NEW SWINDON INTAKE ARE SITTING IN A SEMI-CIRCLE. NEIL IS CHATTING TO THEM AND SHOWING THEM SOME PHOTOS.

BRENT: (to NEIL)
Keeping them occupied for me. The main event. I hope you warmed them up better than last time. Doesn't look like it.

NEIL:
Okay … see you later … Have fun.

THERE IS A CHORUS OF "GOODBYES" FROM THE SWINDON CREW.

BRENT SMILES AND WATCHES NEIL LEAVE.

BRENT:
Anyway, good … Hello. Obviously, I can't give you an appraisal as such – you've only been here a week – but I did want to try to get a flavour of how you're all settling in. I know it's probably not the same vibe that you're used to – Neil ruled with a bit more of an iron fist, I know, than me – but … Settling in, having a good time?

THERE ARE UNCOMMITTED NODS AND SHRUGS.

BRENT:
How is it different?

NO-ONE ANSWERS.

BRENT:
More laid-back presumably?
(POINTING TO A SWINDON EMPLOYEE)
Do you think it's more laid-back?

THE SWINDON EMPLOYEE MUMBLES.

BRENT: (aggressive)
Yes?

SWINDON EMPLOYEE:
Yes.

BRENT:
Say "Yes", then, if you think it's more laid-back. More laid-back, more fun …

TRUDY: (under breath)
Well …

BRENT: (hearing this, agitated)
Uh?

TRUDY:
Nothing.

BRENT:
Go on.

TRUDY:
Well, we're actually used to doing stuff like, working hard, you know, being motivated, but there's not much dynamism out there, is there? I mean people look like they're getting away with murder.

BRENT:
Having a laugh. Yes.

TRUDY:
Well, I think quite a few of us are bored.

PEOPLE NOD IN AGREEMENT.

BRENT:
Oh, what, you preferred Swindon?

SWINDON EMPLOYEE:
More of a laugh.

BRENT:
You're having a laugh, saying that! What's so good about Swindon? Neil?

SWINDON EMPLOYEE:
Yeah, for one.

BRENT:
What? You prefer Neil to me?

THEIR SILENCE SPEAKS VOLUMES.

BRENT:
Who thinks Neil is more of a laugh than me? Hands up.

EVERYONE PUTS UP THEIR HANDS.

BRENT:
That's mental. Come off it. You … We're gonna have a drink, come out for a drink with me and see who's more of a laugh, yeah? Put your money where your mouth is. Right. We'll go for a drink lunchtime. We'll go … Right.

HE RUSHES OUT INTO THE OPEN-PLAN AREA.

BRENT:
Right. Here we are. Right. It's an outing. Okay? Lunchtime. Show that lot what the Slough lot are like. Yeah? Keith, what are you doing lunchtime?

SCENE 16. INT. PUB. DAY.

THE PUB IS ONE OF THOSE NEWISH, PURPOSE-BUILT, INDUSTRIAL-ESTATE PUBS WITH NO ATMOSPHERE.

THREE OF THE SWINDON STAFF ARE SITTING AT THE TABLE. BIG KEITH AND MOUSY SHEILA ARE THE ONLY SLOUGH REGULARS WHO ARE PRESENT.

BRENT COMES OVER CARRYING DRINKS AND DISHES THEM OUT.

BRENT:
Welcome to Alcoholics Anonymous. No. Purely social. I know someone who is an alcoholic and it is no laughing matter, particularly for his wife, so … And she's got alapecia, so not a happy home life. And their eldest is like that Dustin Hoffman in 'Rainman' so, that's probably what turned him to it in the first place.

BRENDA IS LEANING FORWARD TO TAKE A CRISP FROM A PACKET OPEN ON THE TABLE. AS SHE DOES SO, BRENT RUDELY PULLS HER WHEELCHAIR BACKWARDS SO HE CAN GET PAST. SHE'S YANKED AWAY FROM THE CRISPS.

BRENT, IN A CHEERY MOOD, SITS DOWN.

BRENT:
So, looking forward to the weekend? Cheers.

PEOPLE MUTTER "CHEERS", BUT CONVERSATION IS NON-EXISTENT. BRENT POINTS AT HIS PINT OF BEER.

BRENT: (making conversation)
That's a lovely drop of ale, that. That's Courage. You get a lot of that round here … 'cos the, the main brewery's in Reading … so er, they do it all over, they do it in London and everything so, er … What's the brewery in Swindon? Is there a big …

SWINDON EMPLOYEES:
Don't know.

BRENT:
It might be Courage, actually.

SWINDON EMPLOYEE:
I don't know.

BRENT LOOKS ROUND THE PUB.

BRENT:
No, er … This is alright though, innit?

ONE OF THE SWINDON EMPLOYEES POINTS SOMETHING OUT ACROSS THE ROOM TO ONE OF HIS SWINDON COLLEAGUES. THEY WHISPER TO ONE ANOTHER. ONE LAUGHS.

BRENT: (noticing)
Uh?

SWINDON EMPLOYEE:
No. It's just a private joke.

BRENT:
Alright. I was saying, you think this is nice: there's a lovely pub near me, the Gardener's Arms …

THE SWINDON DUO WHISPER TO EACH OTHER AGAIN.

BRENT:
What? What are you doing?

SWINDON EMPLOYEE:
Oh, it's just a bloke over there looks like someone we know …

BRENT: (slighty agitated)
Okay. One at a time. Focus, yeah, so … You get more out of it in the long run. I promise you that. I forgot what I was saying then; that's what happens when you're …

HE'S LOST HIS TRAIN OF THOUGHT. THERE'S A PAINFUL SILENCE.

SCENE 17. INT. SMOKERS' ROOM. DAY.

TIM AND DAWN ARE SITTING IN THE SMOKERS' ROOM, BANTERING, WHILE TIM PRACTISES DARTS. RACHEL COMES IN.

RACHEL:
Hiya.

TIM:
Hi.

RACHEL:
A couple of mates of mine are going down to Yates's –

TIM:
The wine lodge? Classy.

RACHEL:
Well, I was wondering if you would like to come down with us – or not.
(AFTERTHOUGHT)
And you, Dawn, you can bring Lee if you like.

DAWN:
Oh, I don't think we'd be able to –

RACHEL: (interrupting)
Okay.
(TO TIM)
But you can come?

TIM THROWS A SUBTLE LOOK AT DAWN, AS THOUGH GETTING HER PERMISSION. SHE OFFERS LITTLE IN RETURN, SO HE MAKES THE DECISION ON HIS OWN.

TIM:
Yeah, yeah, that'd be great thanks.

RACHEL:
Great. Okay, um …

TIM:
You're talking about tonight.

RACHEL:
Yeah.

TIM:
Yeah, brilliant.

RACHEL:
Yeah, you know just after work or –

TIM:
Yeah, alright, we'll have a couple of drinks. Yeah.

RACHEL:
Cool …

TIM:
Excellent.

RACHEL:
Okay.

TIM:
Good work. See you in a bit, alright.

SHE SMILES, STILL A BIT EMBARRASSED, AND LEAVES AGAIN. TIM AND DAWN SIT IN SILENCE FOR A MOMENT. DAWN BREAKS THE SILENCE.

DAWN:
That'll be fun.

TIM:
Yeah. Yes. Yeah. That will be cool. Cool as a cucumber.

THE SILENCE RESUMES.

SCENE 18. INT. PUB. DAY.

KEITH IS FINISHING EATING A PIE. PEOPLE ARE SITTING IN SILENCE, WATCHING HIM EAT. HE SEEMS TO TAKE FOREVER.

BRENT:
Good?

KEITH:
It was alright.

BRENT:
I've, I've eaten here so … If you want a really good pie, the Gardener's …

YET ANOTHER PREGNANT PAUSE.

BRENT:
This has been a wash-out, hasn't it? I don't know why I bother if no-one else is gonna make the effort, you know …

SWINDON EMPLOYEE:
We have made the effort.

BRENT:
Uh?

SWINDON EMPLOYEE:
We have made the effort.

BRENT:
Yeah, I'm not having a go at you, it's just –
(HE GESTURES AT BRENDA)
– obviously the best people haven't turned up and it's just … I'm gonna shoot off back to the office. See you later.

HE WALKS OFF ABRUPTLY, LEAVING EVERYONE SITTING AT THE TABLE, SPEECHLESS.

SCENE 19. INT. OPEN-PLAN OFFICE. DAY.

BRENT COMES BACK INTO THE OFFICE. A LITTLE GAME OF FRENCH CRICKET IS UNDER WAY. NEIL IS BATTING. TIM, GARETH AND A FEW OTHERS ARE FIELDING. EVERYONE IS LAUGHING AND ENJOYING THEMSELVES. BRENT MAKES A BEE-LINE FOR GARETH.

BRENT:
What you doing?

GARETH:
Having a laugh.

BRENT:
Are you? Pity you couldn't have had a laugh in the pub at lunchtime. Selfish.

GARETH:
What?

BRENT:
Bit dangerous isn't it? In an office. If you want to work, maybe you should work. As it's quarter past two.

NEIL:
Yeah, alright, we're just finishing off now.

BRENT: (mimicking)
"Yeah, we're finishing off." Just want to be popular as the new boss. "Ooh, love me." Pathetic.

BRENT WALKS INTO HIS OFFICE.

NEIL: (taken aback)
Um, right, I think we should call it a day there. Tim, do you want to put those away? Guys, can you go back to work now, please? Sorry about that.

NEIL WALKS INTO BRENT'S OFFICE. WE SPY ON THEM THROUGH THE WINDOW.

NEIL:
David, can I have a word please?

BRENT:
If you want.

NEIL:
I'm confused. I don't know what just happened there, but obviously you've got a problem with something. What is it?

BRENT:
No, time for work, wasn't it? That's what you say. Let's work, instead of mucking around in the office.

NEIL:
You see, your attitude confuses me. If you don't want to tell me what the problem is, then fine, but don't speak to me like that in front of staff, okay, because you're acting like a petulant kid.

BRENT:
Young at heart.

NEIL:
If you've got a problem, come and speak to me, but don't stand out there and embarrass me and yourself, because I will not stand for it, okay? I've been trying to be nice. I've been trying to deal with this situation delicately because I was mildly embarrassed that we were equivalents and now I'm your boss, but that's the deal: live with it. I don't let anyone talk to me the way you just did – not my staff, not my boss, no-one – and certainly not you. Do you understand?

BRENT: (humbled)
Yeah.

NEIL:
Do you understand?

BRENT: (nearly inaudible)
Yes.

NEIL:
Good. Look, you're a good bloke, Dave, and if there's a problem I'd rather we discuss it sensibly than have to have these little chats. Alright?

BRENT:
Yeah.

NEIL:
Shake on it?

BRENT SHAKES NEIL'S HAND.

NEIL:
Great. Thank you.

NEIL EXITS. BRENT WATCHES HIM LEAVE.

SCENE 20. INT. OPEN-PLAN OFFICE. DAY.

NEIL SAYS GOODBYE TO TIM AND GARETH AND LEAVES. BRENT EMERGES FROM HIS OFFICE TO JOIN THEM.

BRENT: (hushed tones, conspiratorial)
Did you hear that? Did you hear any of the conversation in there?

TIM:
No.

BRENT:
I've just had it out with Neil. He showed his true colours, didn't he?

TIM:
What do you mean? He's alright. He seems like a good bloke.

BRENT:
Is that what you think? Oh, I'd better not say anything then. Watch your back.
(HE POINTS TO GARETH)
He was slagging you off.

TIM:
What?

BRENT:
Slagging you off.

GARETH:
What, me personally?

BRENT:
Yeah.

GARETH:
What. Just me?

BRENT:
Yeah.
(POINTS TO TIM)
And you. Slagging all you lot off.

GARETH:
What was he saying?

BRENT:
Just going, "Oh yeah, your lot are rubbish", and that. And I was going, "Our lot are rubbish? Your Swindon lot are shit." And he got aggressive and I went berserk.

GARETH:
Did you hit him?

BRENT:
No. If I had have done, he'd have come through that wall.

TIM:
I don't know, he's pretty trim, mate.

BRENT:
Yeah? Against karate?

TIM:
So, David, what did he actually say about us?

BRENT: (to the huddle)
He was just slagging you lot off. And I went, "Your Swindon lot are little slugs. They're little slugs, with no personality. You're just jealous that we're better at everything than you." I tell you what, on a serious note, if it did kick off between me and him, get out, I don't want you lot getting hurt, it's not worth it.

GARETH:
Well, I'd step in if you want.

BRENT:
No, this would be big boy shit, mate, but cheers ...

GARETH: (demonstrating a move)
Use that one ... Hit them really hard above their ears, it causes a vacuum in their brain, kills them instantly.

BRENT: (slightly manic now)
I wouldn't want him to die. I'd want to keep the little twat alive, with the shit I was gonna pull on him.

HE LEAVES THIS HANGING IN THE AIR AND WALKS OFF.

SCENE 21. INT. KITCHEN. DAY.

RACHEL IS MAKING COFFEE. GARETH APPROACHES.

GARETH:
Alright. Hi.

RACHEL:
Hello.

GARETH:
You don't have a boyfriend do you?

RACHEL:
No.

GARETH:
Any kids from previous marriages or anything?

RACHEL:
Er, no.

GARETH:
Would you like to come out for a drink with me tonight?

RACHEL:
Um, I can't, I'm afraid. I'm gonna go out with Tim, so ...

GARETH:
Tonight?

RACHEL:
Yeah.

GARETH:
Can I come?

RACHEL:
Er, not really.

GARETH:
But you're not planning on getting off with him, or anything?

RACHEL:
Look, I don't think this is any of your business.

GARETH:
No, sorry, it's none of my business. No, you go out, have a drink by all means. Enjoy yourself. Just know that if you don't go all the way with Tim, I will still be interested. Right?

RACHEL:
Thanks, that's, er ... It's good to know I have something to fall back on.

GARETH:
Yeah.

RACHEL: (winding him up)
What if I do go all the way with Tim, but I want a little bit more with you?

GARETH: (oblivious to the sarcasm)
I don't usually do sloppy seconds, but I judge everything on its individual merits. So we'll cross that river when we come to it.

RACHEL:
Thanks. That's good to know.

GARETH:
No problem.

GARETH WALKS OFF. JAMIE ENTERS THE KITCHEN.

JAMIE:
You boiling the kettle?

RACHEL:
Yes, it's actually just boiled so ...

GARETH LEANS BACK INTO THE KITCHEN.

GARETH:
One amendment. If you do go all the way with Tim and you expect me to go in there afterwards –

HE POINTS TO RACHEL'S GROIN. SHE LOOKS DOWN. JAMIE LOOKS DOWN AS WELL.

GARETH:
– make sure he wears a condom. Alright? Sort of a rule.

HE WALKS OFF.

JAMIE CONTINUES TO MAKE COFFEE, RACHEL EMBARRASSED, HE DUMBFOUNDED.

JAMIE: (making conversation)
Is there any milk?

RACHEL:
Yeah. Um, it's in the fridge

SCENE 22. INT. OPEN-PLAN OFFICE. DAY.

BRENT IS SITTING IN HIS OFFICE LOOKING PENSIVE.

DAWN HAS HER COAT ON AND IS SWITCHING OFF HER COMPUTER. TIM AND RACHEL LEAVE TOGETHER – DAWN WATCHES THEM GO.

OTHER PEOPLE ARE LEAVING. DAWN TAKES A FILE IN TO BRENT, CLEARLY ON HER WAY HOME.

BRENT:
Cheers. Oh, can you call Milsons and get that credit breakdown faxed over, or e-mailed, or whatever?

DAWN:
Yep. Sure.

BRENT:
And, er, do you mind typing up those appraisal contracts ASAP? I want to get them back to them.

DAWN:
Sure. Okay. See you Monday.

BRENT:
See you later.

SHE IS ON HER WAY OUT.

BRENT:
Dawn – I'm fed up. I'm fed up, to be honest. It's just I …

THIS SUDDEN OUTBURST CATCHES DAWN STANDING IN LIMBO BETWEEN BRENT AND THE DOOR.

DAWN:
Oh. Why?

BRENT:
This place, I don't say anything … But this place, sometimes I think it's a right shit-hole.

DAWN:
Do you?

BRENT:
Yeah.

PAUSE.

BRENT:
Do you think I'm funny?

DAWN:
Uh-huh. Yep.

BRENT:
Do you think Neil's funny? Sit down.

HE MOTIONS TO A CHAIR. DAWN FEELS OBLIGED TO SIT DOWN.

DAWN:
Do I think Neil's funny? Er ...

BRENT:
Yeah.

DAWN:
I don't really know him, David.

BRENT:
But he's not funnier than me?

DAWN:
No, definitely not.

BRENT:
No. Right. I wish you'd tell that to the Swindon lot – miserable bunch of ... ain't they, some of them? Boring.

DAWN:
Mmm.

BRENT:
What's your favourite stuff that I do, comedy-wise?

DAWN: (bluffing)
Um, oh, there's too much.

BRENT:
Impressions?

DAWN: (leaping on his suggestion)
Oh, yes.

<u>BRENT:</u>
Which ones?

<u>DAWN:</u>
Er, oh … Which ones are there again?

<u>BRENT:</u>
Kermit.

<u>DAWN:</u>
Kermit. Brilliant.

<u>BRENT:</u> (as Kermit the Frog)
"Er, welcome to The Muppet Show."

DAWN FORCES A LAUGH. BRENT LOOKS PLEASED.

<u>BRENT:</u> (as Miss Piggy)
"Hi yah, frog!"

HE SWINGS HIS HAND TOWARDS DAWN'S HEAD, STOPPING JUST SHORT OF GIVING HER A CHOP TO THE NECK.

<u>BRENT:</u>
Miss Piggy. Do you know Kermit's nephew, Robin? Here's one …
(SINGING)
Halfway up the stairs is the stair where I sit …

<u>DAWN:</u>
Do you do Gonzo?

<u>BRENT:</u>
No. Do you want a beer?

<u>DAWN:</u>
Er, I can't go to the pub.

<u>BRENT:</u>
No, no, no, I've got some here. For emergencies.

HE DISAPPEARS BEHIND HIS DESK.

DAWN, STILL IN HER COAT, LOOKS UNCOMFORTABLE.

BRENT REAPPEARS WITH TWO LITTLE BOTTLES OF BEER. HE HANDS ONE TO DAWN AND SHUFFLES HIS CHAIR ROUND TO BE NEXT TO HER.

BRENT:
Cheers … I was looking through some of my old poems I used to do.

DAWN:
Oh, do you –

BRENT:
Yeah.

DAWN:
Oh, I didn't know. Yeah, so what sort of –

BRENT:
Quite, sort of, powerful. Here's one. Shall I read one to you? This one's called 'Excalibur'.
(RECITING LOUDLY)
I froze your tears and made a dagger,
And stabbed it in my cock forever –
It stays there like Excalibur.
Are you my Arthur? Say you are.

DAWN:
Good –

BRENT:
Take this cool dark steelèd blade,
Steal it, sheathe it in your lake.
I'd drown with you to be together.
Must you breathe, 'cause I need heaven.

DAWN:
Ahh, it's … powerful.

BRENT:
Very. And double meanings, did you get the double meanings?

<u>DAWN:</u>
I did.

BRENT SITS BACK AND MUSES ON THINGS. HE ABSENT-MINDEDLY BLOWS INTO HIS BOTTLE TOP. IT MAKES A LITTLE WHISTLING NOISE. DAWN LOOKS ON, UNABLE TO ESCAPE.

<u>CLOSING MUSIC AND END CREDITS, THEN:</u>

DAWN AND BRENT ARE BOTH STILL SITTING IN HIS OFFICE, BLOWING INTO THEIR BOTTLES.

Episode **Three**

CAST
David Brent RICKY GERVAIS
Tim MARTIN FREEMAN
Gareth MACKENZIE CROOK
Dawn LUCY DAVIS
Neil PATRICK BALADI
Rachel STACEY ROCA
Chris Finch RALPH INESON

with
Lee JOEL BECKETT
Trudy RACHEL ISAAC
Ray TOM GOODMAN-HILL
Jude JENNIFER HENNESEY
Keith EWEN MACINTOSH
Oliver HOWARD SADDLER
Glyn DAVID SCHAAL

and
Ben Bradshaw, Jamie Deeks,
Patrick Driver, Julie Fernandez,
Jane Lucas, Tony MacMurray,
Emma Manton, Alexander Perkins
and Philip Pickard

SCENE 1. INT. RECEPTION. DAY.

NEIL IS TALKING JOKINGLY WITH DAWN AT THE RECEPTION DESK. HE IS WEARING HIS CUSTOMARY TAN LEATHER JACKET.

BRENT ARRIVES. HE IS WEARING A TAN LEATHER JACKET LIKE NEIL'S. IT'S LESS FASHIONABLE OR WELL-CUT, BUT OTHERWISE REMARKABLY SIMILAR.

BRENT:
Hiya.

NEIL:
Hiya. Nice jacket.

BRENT:
Whatever.

NEIL:
It's a bit like mine.

BRENT:
What make's yours?

NEIL:
Armani.

BRENT:
Expensive.

NEIL:
And yours?

BRENT: (smug)
Sergio Georgini.

NEIL: (looking down)
New shoes as well. Quite a heel on them.

BRENT: (trying to be cool)
We still on for ten?

NEIL:
Yep.

BRENT HEADS FOR HIS OFFICE, NONCHALANTLY. DAWN GLANCES AT HIS SHOES AS HE WALKS AWAY AND STIFLES A LAUGH.

BRENT TALKING HEAD. INT. DAY.

BRENT:
People see me and they see the suit and they go, "You're not fooling anyone." They know I'm rock 'n' roll through and through, but you know that old thing: "Live fast die young"? Not my way. Live fast? Sure – live too bloody fast sometimes – but die young?

HE SHAKES HIS HEAD.

BRENT:
Die old …

HE LETS THIS HANG IN THE AIR LIKE IT'S THE MOST PROFOUND IDEA EVER.

BRENT:
That's the way I … Not orthodox, you know. I don't live by "the rules". And if there's one other person who's influenced me in that way, I think, someone who is a maverick, someone who does that –
(GIVES THE FINGER)
– to the system, then it's Ian Botham. Because Beefy will happily say –
(MIMES WANKING)
– "That's what I think of your selection policy, yeah? Yes, I've hit the odd copper. Yes, I've enjoyed the odd doobie –
(MIMES SMOKING)
– but will you piss off and leave me alone? I'm walking to John O'Groats for some spastics."

SCENE 2. INT. BRENT'S OFFICE. DAY.

NEIL:
Have you been re-organising stuff out there?

BRENT:
Er, just been –

NEIL:
Just looks a bit chaotic that's all.

BRENT:
– assimilating, re-assimilating and you know –

NEIL:
Re-assimilating what?

BRENT:
Just taking on people and putting them into – Just categorising. Not in any sort of, like – "label me" – but just er, you know, that's your vibe, that's your vibe ...

HE INTERWEAVES HIS FINGERS IN A SMUG WAY.

NEIL:
Uh-huh.

BRENT:
You know.

SCENE 3. INT. OPEN-PLAN OFFICE. DAY.

THERE IS MUCH LAUGHTER AND CHATTER. TRUDY IS UNWRAPPING A BIRTHDAY PRESENT.

TRUDY:
What's in here then? Let's have a look. Oh my God, a leather basque! Fantastic.

GARETH: (subtle)
Try it on –

TRUDY:
I've always wanted one of these actually, a leather basque. Cheers guys.

SHE HOLDS UP THE BASQUE AGAINST HERSELF AND THEN TRIES IT ON OVER HER TOP.

GARETH: (earnest)
You should try it on, try it on properly in case you have to take it back – you should try it on without that stuff on underneath.

TRUDY: (ignoring GARETH)
It fits!

RACHEL HANDS TRUDY ANOTHER GIFT. TRUDY OPENS IT. IT IS A HUGE, OVERSIZED PINK DILDO. EVERYONE LAUGHS.

TRUDY:
Oh my God, it's disgusting. You dirty …

THERE IS SOME GENERAL BAWDY BANTER. TIM TAKES THE DILDO AND WAVES IT AT GARETH.

TIM:
Can I just, sorry … Look at the face, look at the face, Gareth, look at the face!

GARETH:
Eugh, I can't believe you're even touching that!

TIM:
Why?

GARETH:
It's disgusting.

TIM:
It's not disgusting.

TIM WIGGLES IT IN GARETH'S FACE.

GARETH:
You don't know where that's been, mate.

TIM:
Well, I do know where it's … It's been in a box, Gareth.

GARETH:
No, I mean at the factory, you don't know what goes on at the factory …

TIM:
The factory, your amazing mind again.

GARETH:
No, in my experience women who work in factories are slappers, so …

EVERYONE REACTS.

TRUDY: (laughing)
Thank you everybody for my lovely presents.

SCENE 4. INT. BRENT'S OFFICE. DAY.

BRENT AND NEIL ARE STILL TALKING.

BRENT:
They're malleable and you know, that's what I like really. I don't like people coming here with, "Oh, we did it this way, we did it that way." I just want to go, "Do it this way – if you like. If you don't … " Team playing. I call it "team individuality". It's a new … It's like a management style. Again, guilty, unorthodox – sue me.

NEIL:
It certainly is, yeah. How does that work?

BRENT:
But you know, nothing ever changes by staying the same. Quite literally.

SCENE 5. INT. OPEN-PLAN OFFICE/BRENT'S OFFICE. DAY.

TIM IS WORKING. HE HAS THE DILDO STANDING UPRIGHT ON HIS DESK. GARETH IS ALSO WORKING. RACHEL WALKS UP TO TIM, LOOKING BORED. SHE PICKS UP THE DILDO.

TIM:
Hello.

GARETH:
Alright.

RACHEL:
You like that, don't you?

TIM:
What?

RACHEL:
Is that because it looks like yours?

TIM:
Yeah. It's identical. Well, mine's not that size, it's very, very tiny, but it is made of plastic.

GARETH: (trying to flirt)
Mine's massive and it ain't made of plastic.

HE CHUCKLES AT HIS OWN STUNNINGLY WITTY COMMENT.

RACHEL: (to TIM)
I dare you to go and put it in Brent's office.

TIM:
Why?

RACHEL:
It's a dare.

TIM:
Yeah, I know, but he's having a meeting with Neil, I can't …

RACHEL:
Well, that's kind of the challenge, mate.

TIM:
Well, why would I do that?

RACHEL:
'Cos it'll make me laugh.

GARETH:
I'll do it.

TIM:
No, I'll do it. It's alright.

RACHEL:
Look, all you've got to do is just go in there and hide it in there somewhere, that's all.

TIM:
Just hide it?

RACHEL:
Yeah.

TIM:
Simple. It couldn't be easier. Straightforward.

TIM PICKS UP THE DILDO AND MAKES HIS WAY TOWARDS BRENT'S OFFICE. BRENT AND NEIL ARE INSIDE HAVING A MEETING. TIM KNOCKS AND GOES IN WITH THE DILDO BEHIND HIS BACK.

BRENT:
Come in.

TIM:
Sorry to interrupt. I just wondered if … That's embarrassing, I've completely forgotten what I came in for … Oh, I'm sorry …

HE 'ABSENT-MINDEDLY' PICKS UP A FOLDER AND HIDES THE DILDO BEHIND IT.

BRENT:
That's alright.

TIM:
Um, it's gone. Come on, come on Tim, get it back, no …

BRENT:
Too many late nights.

TIM:
Oh no, sorry, it's totally gone.

BRENT:
Don't worry about it.

TIM:
I'm holding your folder.

TIM PUTS THE FOLDER BACK ON BRENT'S DESK, WITH THE DILDO HIDDEN UNDERNEATH.

TIM:
Sorry. I'm just … No, it's gone. BSE.

BRENT:
Don't worry. Come back.

TIM:
No more beef.

NEIL:
As you're here, there's something you can do for me. My lot haven't even been down to the warehouse yet.

TIM:
Okay.

NEIL:
It would be … Would you mind taking them down, just familiarise them?

<u>BRENT:</u> (annoyed)
There's not a lot of point, there's not a lot to see.

<u>NEIL:</u>
You know, we're one organisation. I think it'd be quite a good idea for everyone to know everyone else.
(TO TIM)
If you just tell Glyn I said it was okay.

<u>TIM:</u>
Brilliant.

<u>BRENT:</u> (to TIM)
Well, tell Taffy that I said it was okay, and that Neil agrees with me – the Brentosaurus Rex.

<u>TIM:</u>
Okay.

<u>NEIL:</u>
Thanks.

HE WALKS BACK OUT, LAUGHING. RACHEL IS IMPRESSED; GARETH, OF COURSE, IS NOT.

<u>TIM:</u>
Sorry, that was brilliant.

<u>RACHEL:</u>
That was, absolutely –

<u>TIM:</u>
Did you see where it went, it went under the folder.

THEY SLAP HANDS, CONGRATULATING EACH OTHER. WE SEE DAWN, WATCHING FROM RECEPTION, AS RACHEL AND TIM BUMP THEIR HIPS TOGETHER.

<u>TIM:</u>
Gareth, out of ten?

GARETH:
I give it a three.

TIM:
Three?

RACHEL:
Three.

SCENE 6. INT. SMOKERS' ROOM. DAY.

OLIVER AND ANOTHER SWINDON EMPLOYEE ARE PLAYING DARTS.

BRENT SUDDENLY LEANS INTO SHOT.

BRENT: (to camera)
"You can't beat a bit of bully!"
Bullseye. Here they are. Likely lads.

EMPLOYEE:
New shoes.

BRENT: (shrugging)
Fashion.

EMPLOYEE:
Do you want a go?

BRENT: (acting casual)
Yeah. Up to the oche, let Tony look after you. Oh dear, nothing in this game for two in a bed.

HE TAKES A DART, AIMS AND THROWS IT.

IT DISAPPEARS OFF-SCREEN BUT WE HEAR IT BANG AGAINST THE BOARD AND CLATTER LOUDLY TO THE GROUND.

BRENT:
Shit flights on those, aren't they? No wonder. Bit fuddy-duddy, darts, isn't it, for a couple of young lads your age?

EMPLOYEE:
I'm not young, I'm twenty-nine.

BRENT:
Ooh, over the hill. How old would you say I was, if you didn't know me?

EMPLOYEE:
Um ... forty?

BRENT:
No, how old do you think I look?

EMPLOYEE:
Thirty-nine?

BRENT: (scoffing, annoyed)
Most people think I look about thirty.

EMPLOYEE:
Definitely not.

BRENT:
Oh, are you calling them liars?
(TO OLIVER)
What do you think?

OLIVER:
Well, between 30 and 40?

BRENT: (nodding)
Yes. More honest.

HIS POINT MADE, BRENT LEAVES.

SCENE 6. EXT. WAREHOUSE OUTER DOOR. DAY.

TIM IS LEADING THE SWINDON GANG INTO THE WAREHOUSE. HE STOPS OUTSIDE THE MAIN DOOR.

TIM:
Okay, now guys we're about to enter a warehouse environment. Now, I must warn you that some of the people in here will be working class, so there may be arse cleavage. So, just find a partner, hold hands, don't talk to anyone though, okay? Are you chewing? Right, okay. Let's go.

THEY LAUGH AS HE LEADS THEM INSIDE.

SCENE 7. INT. WAREHOUSE. DAY.

THERE IS MUCH WAREHOUSE HUBBUB.

TIM LEADS THE GROUP FURTHER INSIDE. A FEW WORKMEN ARE HAVING A BREAK. DAWN IS ALSO THERE, HAVING A COFFEE WITH HER FIANCE LEE. THERE IS A VAGUELY THREATENING AIR IN THE WAREHOUSE, AS IF THE WHITE-COLLAR WORKERS AREN'T QUITE WELCOME IN THIS BLUE-COLLAR WORLD.

TIM:
Here we are, here's the hub of the operation, working hard as usual. Alright?

GLYN:
The strippers have arrived.

TIM: (unbuttoning his shirt)
Well, I tell you what Glyn, you can have five minutes, but no touching.

GLYN:
I always knew you were bent.

LEE SQUEEZES ONE OF DAWN'S BREASTS.

LEE:
Hey, don't worry. She'll get the old milkers out for a tenner.

HIS WORKMATES CACKLE WITH LAUGHTER. DAWN ROUNDS ON LEE, FURIOUS.

DAWN:
Fuck off.

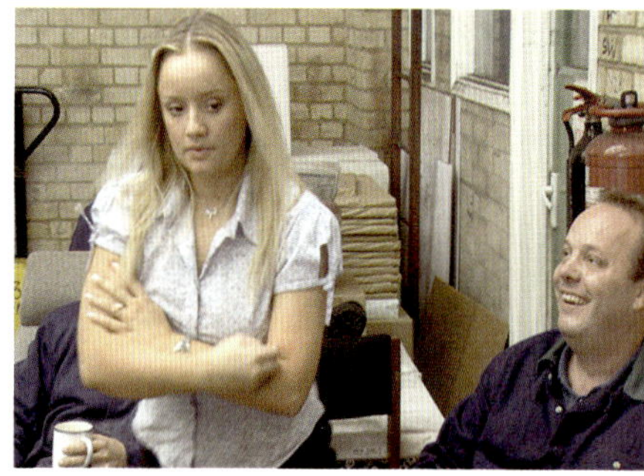

LEE:
What?

SHE GETS UP AND WALKS OFF. LEE'S WORKMATES LAUGH. TIM LOOKS FRUSTRATED, KNOWING NOW IS NOT THE TIME TO SPRING TO DAWN'S DEFENCE.

GLYN:
Oi, lend us a tenner.

WAREHOUSE MAN: (to LEE)
You won't be seeing them tonight.

LEE:
That's alright. I got cable …

HIS WORKMATES LAUGH.

TIM AND THE SWINDON PEOPLE JUST LOOK EMBARRASSED.

TIM:
Okay, um, I'm going to show you this aisle first.

WAREHOUSE MAN: (shouting to TIM)
Bender!

SCENE 9. INT. OPEN-PLAN OFFICE. DAY

TRUDY IS CLEARLY ENJOYING HER BIRTHDAY AND IS NOT HARD AT WORK.

TRUDY: (on phone)
No, get lost you cheeky bastard. Ha ha ha! … No! … Ha ha ha!

SCENE 10. INT. OPEN-PLAN OFFICE. DAY

BRENT IS COMING BACK INTO THE OFFICE, STILL WEARING HIS NEW LEATHER JACKET. A MIDDLE-AGED MAN AND AN ATTRACTIVE THIRTY-SOMETHING WOMAN ARE SITTING WAITING FOR HIM.

DAWN POINTS THEM OUT.

DAWN:
David, this is Ray and Jude.

BRENT:
Who?

DAWN:
Ray and Jude from – sorry, forgotten where you're from.

RAY: (getting up)
From Cooper and Webb Consultants.

BRENT: (jokey)
Who's Cooper and who's Webb?

RAY:
Neither of us.

BRENT:
Bet you get that all the time, do you?

RAY:
No.

RAY OPENS HIS FOLDER.

RAY:
Anyway, er …

BRENT TURNS HIS BACK ON HIM.

BRENT:
First things first. Any more mail?

DAWN HANDS HIM SOME POST.

BRENT:
Mr D. Brent – that's me.

HE LOOKS THROUGH THE POST VERY DELIBERATELY, KEEPING HIS VISITORS WAITING. RAY AND JUDE STAND THERE AWKWARDLY.

BRENT LEAVES THE MAIL AND STARTS TO WALK TOWARDS HIS OFFICE.

BRENT:
Come through.

THEY FOLLOW HIM INTO HIS OFFICE. BRENT REMOVES HIS JACKET WITH A FLOURISH. DAWN CAN'T RESIST ANOTHER SMILE WHEN SHE SEES HIS SHOES.

SCENE 11. INT. BRENT'S OFFICE. DAY.

BRENT HANGS UP HIS JACKET AND EASES HIMSELF BEHIND HIS DESK. RAY AND JUDE ARE LEFT TO FIND CHAIRS FOR THEMSELVES.

BRENT:
Must, just er …

HE PICKS UP THE PHONE-RECEIVER AND FIDDLES WITH HIS COMPUTER – HE'S JUST TRYING TO LOOK BUSY.

BRENT:
Shoot.

RAY:
Well, are you aware of what we do?

BRENT:
Nooo.

RAY:
Basically we organise training days for corporations and individuals who pay to get an advantage in business. But it's not just telling them boring facts, we also have business experts who train them on how to act, how to walk into a room and say, "I'm the guy you're going to do business with."

BRENT:
Okay, I'm going to stop you there. I really don't need anything like that. I do all my own in-house training –

RAY:
Sorry, no, no, sorry, we're not trying to get your business; we'd very much like you to be one of our experts.

BRENT'S ATTITUDE CHANGES FROM SHOWING OFF TO SELF-CONGRATULATORY.

BRENT:
Good choice, why'd you dudes swing by here in the first place?

RAY:
Well, we'd heard a lot of good things about Wernham Hogg. We also got your name from a guy we've worked with called Andy Hitchcock.

BRENT:
Oh God. Oh no, Cockles. Cocky. The Big Cock. Next time you're talking to him, just ask him if he got the grass stains out of his trousers. Not in front of his wife, 'cos … 'cos …

HE SUDDENLY REMEMBERS HE'S ON CAMERA AND LOOKS SHEEPISH. HE'S OBVIOUSLY JUST REVEALED SOME MAJOR MARITAL INFIDELITY ON TELEVISION, AND MOVES ON QUICKLY.

BRENT:
What sort of tip would you want me on if I was to … ?

RAY:
We're looking for people who are dynamic but who are also good communicators,

BRENT:
Sure.

RAY:
It's a corporate message but obviously we're after people who can communicate with young people, with twenty-somethings.

BRENT PUTS HIS LEGS UP ONTO THE DESK – HE'S CLEARLY TRYING TO SHOW OFF HIS NEW SHOES.

THEY ARE GARISH, INAPPROPRIATE, SHINY SLIP-ON SHOES WITH A NOTICEABLE CUBAN HEEL.

RAY:
You don't see heels like those much nowadays.

BRENT:
You can still find 'em. Um, what sort of 'bunce' would I be looking at?

RAY:
Sorry?

BRENT MIMES FINGERING SOME MONEY.

RAY:
Well, to start with –

BRENT: (interrupting)
Bunsen burner.
(EXPLAINING)
Bunsen burner, nice little earner, hence the –

HE LOOKS AT JUDE, SMILING, TRYING TO IMPRESS WITH HIS JARGON.

BRENT:
– bunce.

RAY:
Well, to begin with we'd put you on about three hundred pounds.

BRENT: (taken aback)
Three hundred pounds? Just for an hour's work?

JUDE:
Well, no, you'd only talk for about fifteen minutes.

BRENT: (giggles)
Fifteen minutes. That's, that's twelve hundred pounds an hour, pro rata.
(TO CAMERA)
That's the sort of fee I'd be looking at for this so, you know … Yeah.
(TO RAY AND JUDE)
When would you want to do it?

JUDE:
Well, soon.

BRENT:
Count me in. Thank you.

JUDE:
Sorry, do you have a diary? We could make some dates now.

BRENT:
Absolument.

BRENT PICKS UP HIS DIARY FROM THE DESK. THE BIG PINK DILDO IS UNDERNEATH IT.

BRENT:
What's that?

<u>JUDE:</u>
It's a dildo.

<u>BRENT:</u> (fazed)
Is it yours?

<u>JUDE:</u> (insulted)
No.

<u>BRENT:</u>
No, no, well, well, I dunno. Sorry. This is an example of … problems. Let's have a look.

BRENT PICKS UP THE DILDO AND GOES OUT TO ADDRESS HIS TEAM. RAY AND JUDE FOLLOW HIM OUT.

<u>BRENT:</u>
Okay, everybody. What am I doing in there with a dildo?

PEOPLE REACT.

<u>BRENT:</u> (pointing to JUDE)
She says it's not hers, and I for one believe her.

HE'S POINTING AT JUDE WITH THE DILDO. IT'S A BIT TOO CLOSE TO HER FACE TO BE POLITE.

<u>BRENT:</u>
So whose is it?

TRUDY PUTS HER HAND UP.

<u>BRENT:</u>
Right. What's it doing in there?

<u>TRUDY:</u>
Well, it's a birthday present, but I don't know what it's doing in there.

<u>BRENT:</u>
Birthday, so … Good harmless fun, but you know … Is it today, your birthday? Many happy returns. But, what have we learnt from this?

TRUDY:
Not to leave your dildo lying round?

BRENT:
Don't let it out of your sight, because it can wind up anywhere, and it's ... Oh, what's that?

HE HAS ACCIDENTALLY TRIGGERED THE SWITCH ON THE DILDO. IT STARTS TO MOVE AROUND IN HIS HAND, LEAVING LITTLE TO THE IMAGINATION.

BRENT: (embarrassed)
Sorry, how d'you ... ? Oh, it's worse.

THE VIBRATIONS ACCELERATE.

BRENT:
What do you do when that happens? Well, you probably ... Can you get that, make sure that gets back to ...

EMBARRASSED, HE HURRIEDLY HANDS IT TO TIM.

BRENT:
Yes, sure, yeah. We were actually in the middle of something, so, and that ...

HE TRAILS OFF AND TAKES RAY AND JUDE BACK INSIDE HIS OFFICE.

TIM WAVES THE DILDO IN GARETH'S FACE AGAIN.

SCENE 12. INT. OPEN-PLAN OFFICE. DAY.

RACHEL AND TIM ARE TRYING TO THINK OF MORE OFFICE PRANKS.

TIM:
You've got to smuggle this somewhere about your person. I'm not saying anything about it, you've got to ...

RACHEL:
What does that mean, "about your person"?

TIM:
You've got to –

GARETH:
Oi, if you want to see bravery, come to me, I'll do a dare.

TIM:
Bravery?

GARETH:
Yeah, come on.

TIM:
Oh yeah.

RACHEL:
Okay, okay, no, alright, okay – I'm gonna phone Dav–, no I'm gonna write things for you to say – come here – and then I'm going to phone David and I want you to say exactly what I write down, okay?

GARETH:
No way, you'll make me sound like a bender.

RACHEL:
No, look, I swear I won't. It'll just be, it'll just be funny things –

GARETH:
No way.

RACHEL:
– that'll come out cute and that. Come on Gareth.

GARETH:
I'm not gonna say anything that makes me sound like a bender.

SHE DIALS BRENT'S NUMBER. THEY PUT IT ON SPEAKER-PHONE. IT RINGS THEN WE HEAR BRENT'S VOICE.

BRENT:
Hello?

GARETH:
Hi, it's Gareth.

BRENT:
Hiya. I'm in a meeting at the moment, Gareth.

GARETH:
Yeah, um, I'm just gonna say a few things.

BRENT:
Right.

RACHEL HAS WRITTEN SOMETHING ON A PIECE OF PAPER AND SHE SHOWS IT TO GARETH.

GARETH:
You're doing a great job.

BRENT:
Okay.
(TO RAY AND JUDE)
Just an employee saying what a superb job I'm doing.
(TO GARETH)
Is that it?

GARETH:
No.

SHE SHOWS HIM THE PIECE OF PAPER.

GARETH:
I like your little beard.

BRENT:
Okay. Is that it?

RACHEL HOLDS UP ONE FINGER.

GARETH:
One more thing.

BRENT:
What?

GARETH: (reading what she's written)
You should wear tighter trousers.

RACHEL AND TIM STIFLE LAUGHTER.

BRENT:
Can I give you a call back?

GARETH:
Yep. Bye.

GARETH HANGS UP. RACHEL AND TIM CRACK UP.

TIM: (to RACHEL)
That was genius!

GARETH:
Thank you.

TIM: (still addressing RACHEL)
Genius! Genius!

GARETH LAUGHS, THINKING HE'S PART OF THE FUN. WE SEE DAWN LOOKING AT THE MERRIMENT. TIM AND RACHEL SHARE A HUG. GARETH WATCHES THIS AND AWKWARDLY PUTS HIS ARM ROUND HER.

GARETH:
Brilliant.

SCENE 13. INT. BRENT'S OFFICE. DAY.

RAY AND JUDE ARE STILL WITH BRENT.

JUDE:
We have a website with profiles of all our speakers on it: would you mind answering a few questions?

BRENT:
No. Go for it.

JUDE:
Okay.
(FILLING IN FORM)
If you could have a working lunch with anyone, living or dead, who would it be?

BRENT MUSES ON THIS.

BRENT:
Martin Luther King and the Dalai Lama – and Rory Bremner, just to … 'Cos they could get a bit heavy, couldn't they, the two of them, and he'd lighten things up. Probably do impressions of them. And me.

JUDE:
What's your biggest disappointment?

BRENT:
Alton Towers.

JUDE: (expecting something a bit more profound)
Oh. I've never been.

BRENT:
It's rubbish. Next.

SCENE 14. INT. OPEN-PLAN OFFICE. DAY.

DAWN COMES OVER TO TIM.

TIM:
Hiya.

DAWN:
Still doing practical jokes?

TIM:
No, I'm trying to do some work now. Should be giving them a rest.

DAWN:
Oh, no, I've got some …

TIM:
Really?

DAWN:
Yeah.

TIM:
What you got?

DAWN:
Oh. I used to do loads … Oh, what were they … ? Ah, you know, we can, we can think of some …

TIM:
We can, yeah, absolutely.

DAWN:
Some new ones.

TIM:
Yeah, okay. Let's think of some good ones.

DAWN:
For?

TIM:
For … What about Gareth?

DAWN:
Um, possibly.

TIM:
It's about time he had some tricks played on him.

SCENE 15. INT. BRENT'S OFFICE. DAY.

JUDE:
What would your motto be?

MORE MUSING.

BRENT:
Well, I've noticed that some bosses are intimidated by training their staff up too well, they don't ... I don't mind it. I actually like my staff to be better than me. That way, it keeps me on my toes. So my motto would be: "Be careful 'cos there's always someone ready to step into your shoes and do your job better ... than ... you ... do it."

RAY STARES AT BRENT, DIGESTING HIS PROFUNDITY.

SCENE 16. INT. OPEN-PLAN OFFICE. DAY.

TIM IS MEDDLING WITH GARETH'S TELEPHONE. HE IS GLUING THE HANDSET TO THE PHONE ITSELF. DAWN IS WATCHING HIM, SMIRKING.

TIM:
Heh heh. I'm gluing the phone in the name of fun.

SCENE 17. INT. OPEN-PLAN OFFICE. DAY.

THERE IS SOME REVELRY GOING ON AT RECEPTION. PEOPLE ARE CHATTERING AND LAUGHING. NEIL IS HANDING OUT PLATES OF CAKE.

BRENT APPEARS FROM HIS OFFICE WITH RAY AND JUDE.

<u>**BRENT:**</u>
What's this?

<u>**OLIVER:**</u>
Sorry, it's just a little birthday bash for Trudy. It's her birthday.

<u>**BRENT:**</u>
Who organised this?

<u>**NEIL:**</u>
I did.

NEIL HANDS A SLICE OF CAKE TO BRENT.

<u>**BRENT:**</u> (aside, to RAY and JUDE)
A bit over the top innit?
(TO NEIL)
How much did that cost you? We're paying you too much.

<u>**NEIL:**</u>
No, I made it myself.

BRENT LOOKS SICK.

<u>**SLOUGH EMPLOYEE:**</u> (impressed)
You made it yourself?

<u>**OLIVER:**</u>
Every year he makes them.

BRENT TASTES THE CAKE.

<u>**BRENT:**</u>
Oh, a bit sweet innit? Too rich.

EVERYONE ELSE MAKES "YUMMY" NOISES.

<u>**BRENT:**</u> (pronouncing to no-one)
I prefer a flan.

THIS BRIEFLY STOPS THE MERRIMENT.

SCENE 18. INT. RECEPTION AREA. DAY.

A LITTLE DRINKS PARTY IS UNDER WAY. TIM IS TALKING TO RACHEL. A COUPLE OF SWINDON PEOPLE ARE STANDING CHATTING. WE SEE BRENT SNEAKING BEHIND THEM. HE SIDLES UP.

BRENT:
You look like you're in a meeting. No, it's just that I've just had an interesting meeting.
(POINTING OUT RAY)
You see those two people over there? They're business people and er … quite important actually … And they've got a business and they arrange seminars, management training seminars, where they get expert speakers to come and train … Sort of John Harvey-Jones-type figures. They've asked me, so … Yeah.

HE GRINS SMUGLY AT THE SWINDON PEOPLE. THEY NOD POLITELY BUT NO-ONE'S INTERESTED.

BRENT:
That's perfect for me though, 'cos not only do I know about that stuff – I've got sort of natural authority with people – but I'm an all-round entertainer. So they've –

HE SLOWLY AND POMPOUSLY INTERWEAVES HIS FINGERS.

BRENT:
– those qualities. Keep it under your hat.

HE STROLLS AWAY, CERTAIN THAT HE'S IMPRESSED THEM. HE POUNCES ON SOME MORE UNSUSPECTING EMPLOYEES.

BRENT:
Hey, see those two business people over there …

SCENE 19. INT. OPEN-PLAN OFFICE. DAY.

TIM AND DAWN ARE AT TIM'S DESK. TIM CALLS GARETH'S PHONE. GARETH WALKS OVER AND TRIES TO ANSWER IT. THE WHOLE PHONE COMES UP WITH THE HANDSET AND FLIES ACROSS THE DESK.

TIM AND DAWN BURST INTO LAUGHTER.

GARETH:
Was that you? You're funny. You could have had my eye out.

HIS PHONE IS STILL RINGING. GARETH PRIES IT APART AND SPEAKS INTO THE HANDSET.

GARETH:
Hello. Gareth Keenan.

TIM CAN'T BELIEVE HIS LUCK.

TIM:
Cock! Thank you. Thank you, oh, glorious!

RACHEL COMES BOUNDING OVER. SHE'S LAUGHING AND SHE'S TOO ENTHUSIASTIC, ACTING LIKE SHE WAS PART OF THE JOKE.

TIM:
Did you see that, he still picked it up!

RACHEL:
Was that you?

TIM:
Did you see him? We glued it …

RACHEL:
Was that the superglue? Oh my God.

DAWN REACTS TO THIS. HER EXPRESSION SEEMS TO SAY, "SO HERE SHE IS AGAIN ..."

SCENE 20. INT. OPEN-PLAN OFFICE. DAY.

NEIL IS TALKING TO RAY AND JUDE. BRENT SLOPES UP.

RAY:
Obviously we wouldn't take up very much of your time, we just sort of –

NEIL:
I really appreciate it, your interest, but I'm just so busy at the moment.

BRENT:
What we talking about? What we talking about?

RAY:
We're just trying to involve this chap in motivation. He seems to know what he's talking about.

BRENT: (annoyed)
Oh, after you've asked me, it's a bit rude innit? A bit rude.

RAY:
Oh no, we'd use both of you for different seminars –

BRENT: (anxious)
I can do them both.

NEIL:
Well, I can't do it anyway.

BRENT:
He can't do it anyway.

RAY:
Well, can I have your card just in case?

BRENT:
No point, is there?

JUDE:
Well we might be able to persuade you.

<u>BRENT:</u> (overly aggressive)
Well, he said no once. If he goes back on that, he's weak, so ...

AWKWARD PAUSE.

<u>RAY:</u>
Well, anyway, we ought to be going really.

<u>BRENT:</u>
Yeah, leave it as agreed. Okay.

<u>RAY:</u>
We'll be in touch, David. Nice to meet you.

<u>NEIL:</u>
Nice to meet you. Bye.

<u>BRENT:</u>
Bye. Okay.

THEY LEAVE. BRENT IS LEFT WITH NEIL.

<u>BRENT:</u>
Oh, so you're definitely not doing it. You said no, so ... I thought you were trying to worm your way in.

<u>NEIL:</u> (trying to be nice)
No, I'm not interested.

<u>BRENT:</u> (annoyed)
Why? Beneath you, is it?

<u>NEIL:</u>
No, I just don't think you can teach people that sort of thing. Either you can do it or you can't.

<u>BRENT:</u>
Depends who the guru is.

HE POINTS TO HIMSELF.

<u>NEIL:</u> (jokey)
Beware of false prophets.

BRENT:
No, that's my point, innit? It's not all about profits …

NEIL:
I meant "prophets" as in –

BRENT: (childish)
"I meant, I meant, I meant". "If only, if only." "If only my auntie had bollocks she'd be my uncle" –

BRENT WALKS AWAY.

SCENE 21. INT. OPEN-PLAN OFFICE. DAY.

THE PARTY IS IN FULL SWING. TRUDY SEEMS TO BE DRINKING A LOT.

RACHEL IS SITTING ON TIM'S DESK WITH A PACK OF TOP TRUMPS. THEY ARE BANTERING FLIRTATIOUSLY. TIM'S TALKING HEAD BEGINS OVER THIS.

TIM TALKING HEAD. INT. DAY.

TIM:
No, I don't talk about my love life for a very good reason and that reason is I don't have one. Which is good news for the ladies, I suppose, I am still available. I'm a heck of a catch 'cos, well, let's look at it, I live in Slough … in a lovely house … with my parents. I have my own room which I've had since – yeah, since I was born. That's seen a lot of action, I tell you. Mainly dusting, but er … I went to university for a year as well, before I dropped out, so I'm a quitter, so yeah: form an orderly queue, ladies.

SCENE 22. INT. OPEN-PLAN OFFICE. DAY.

TIM AND RACHEL ARE PLAYING TOP TRUMPS AND FLIRTING. RACHEL IS GETTING MORE PHYSICAL WITH TIM, TOUCHING HIM AND FALLING TOWARDS HIM. DAWN HAS NOTICED THIS.

TIM:
Number of haircuts: is that a valid thing? Are you getting mullered?

RACHEL:
Not really.

TIM:
Right, you've spilled some on your …

HE WHISTLES EUPHEMISTICALLY.

RACHEL:
Yeah, I know I have.

GARETH GLANCES OVER JEALOUSLY.

RACHEL:
Shall we carry on with the game please?

TIM:
I want to carry on. I wish you would. Shoot.

RACHEL STARTS FLICKING THE CARDS ON HIS CHIN.

SCENE 23. INT. OPEN-PLAN OFFICE. DAY.

BRENT IS TRYING TO IMPRESS YET ANOTHER EMPLOYEE, JAMIE.

BRENT:
But if they want to pay me that for fifteen minutes' work that is their prerogative, so I'm not … Oh sorry.

HIS MOBILE PHONE RINGS AND HE ANSWERS IT.

BRENT: (to JAMIE)
Chris Finch.
(INTO PHONE)
Finchy! Alright ... Go on ... "What's the difference between a fox and a dog?" Go on ... Ha ha! "About eight pints of lager"! It's party time here mate. You coming in?

AS HE IS TALKING WE SEE CHRIS FINCH CREEPING INTO THE OFFICE, WHISPERING INTO HIS MOBILE.

BRENT: (oblivious)
You coming in ... ? Why not?

FINCH: (yelling in BRENT's ear)
'Cause I'm already here, you fat twat.

BRENT REELS IN SHOCK. EVERYONE LAUGHS, INCLUDING NEIL.

BRENT: (to NEIL)
Hey Finchy. Chris Finch. Here he is. Neil, a very good friend: Chris Finch.

NEIL:
Yeah, I know Chris, he nicks all my jokes.

FINCH:
I do not nick 'em, I borrow 'em.

THEY SHAKE HANDS IN A STREETWISE STYLE.

FINCH:
Hey, has that Lisa moved up here?

NEIL:
No, she left. She's looking for a job.

FINCH:
Well, if it's a blow job I can help her.

NEIL:
She's not that desperate for money.

FINCH:
Tell her I'll take her up the "dole office".

HE MIMES SHAGGING. BRENT LAUGHS.

NEIL:
The "dole orifice".

BRENT:
Rubbish.

BRENT TURNS UP HIS NOSE AT THIS, BUT FINCH LAUGHS. THIS ANNOYS BRENT.

FINCH:
Well, I've got a vacancy she can fill.

BRENT:
That's better. His work. Don't try and …

SCENE 24. INT. OPEN-PLAN OFFICE. DAY.

THE PARTY CONTINUES. TRUDY IS POURING HERSELF ANOTHER DRINK AND CHATTING TO OLIVER.

WE SEE NEIL AND FINCH. THEY ARE CHATTING LIKE OLD FRIENDS.

RACHEL IS SITTING LOOKING THROUGH THE TOP-TRUMPS CARDS. GARETH CORNERS HER.

GARETH:
If you like Top Trumps you should come to me. I've got about five different sets. Don't try and beat me on Monster Trucks, though, 'cos you won't. My speciality.

RACHEL:
Yeah, it's a game of chance though, isn't it? It's what you –

GARETH:
– No it's not. I would know what cards you've got immediately just through which cards I've got. I used to play it just by myself, with a dummy hand just testing out every different scenario of which cards would beat which other cards, for hours, sometimes three or four hours at a time. But, put in the work, the rewards are obvious.

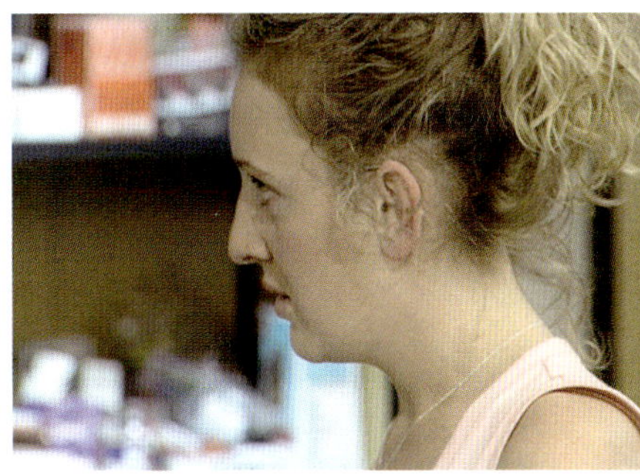

SHE STARES BLANKLY AT HIM.

GARETH:
So I'd know exactly what card you've got in your hand from what cards I've got and I would know, probability-wise, exactly what feature to pick on my card to defeat, statistically, any card that you could have in your hand at that precise moment. You will never win.

SHE STARES AT HIM.

GARETH:
Could still be fun though.

SCENE 25. INT. OPEN-PLAN OFFICE. DAY.

BRENT IS TRYING TO IMPRESS BIG KEITH. FINCH AND ANOTHER EMPLOYEE ARE STANDING NEARBY.

BRENT:
Do you know what I'm getting for, what they're paying me for this?

KEITH:
No.

BRENT:
Fifteen minutes' work, yeah? Three hundred quid. So –

KEITH:
– Twelve hundred quid an hour.

BRENT:
You do the math.

KEITH:
Yeah, it'd be twelve hundred quid an hour.

BRENT:
So that's the sort of …

TRUDY COMES UP TO THEM.

TRUDY:
Can I have a birthday kiss please?

EMPLOYEE:
You certainly can.

SHE KISSES THE EMPLOYEE ON THE LIPS, THEN MOVES ON TO FINCH.

FINCH:
Alright. No tongues.

SHE KISSES FINCH, THEN MOVES ON TO BIG KEITH, BUT THEN STRAIGHT PAST BRENT, WHO HAD BEEN EAGERLY AWAITING HIS KISS.

BRENT:
Oh, that's, that's good, innit? She didn't ask me out of respect. Knows I'd say "No". Good. She didn't cross a boundary and that's, that's … you know … Good girl.

SCENE 26. INT. OPEN-PLAN OFFICE. DAY.

TRUDY, DRINK IN HAND, IS SITTING ON OLIVER'S LAP. HE'S BOUNCING HER UP AND DOWN.

FINCH PASSES BY.

FINCH:
That's a good idea. I always do them from behind if I don't like their face.

TRUDY:
Ooh, cheeky bastard.
(TO OLIVER)
You like my face, don't you, love?

OLIVER:
I love your face. I think you're beautiful.

TRUDY:
Well, you can still do me from behind anyway.

OLIVER:
Oh, I'll bear that in mind then.

THEY BOTH LAUGH. OLIVER CARRIES ON TALKING TO SOMEONE ELSE.

GARETH, WHO HAS OVERHEARD ALL THIS, LEANS DOWN TO SPEAK TO TRUDY.

GARETH:
I'll do you from behind if you want – if it's just a quick in and out, no strings attached.

TRUDY:
That's really sweet. Why don't you put that in an e-mail to me?

GARETH: (nodding)
Alright.

HE WALKS AWAY, CONGRATULATING HIMSELF ON HIS SUCCESS WITH THE LADIES.

SCENE 27. INT. OPEN-PLAN OFFICE. DAY.

THE PARTY IS IN FULL SWING. FINCH AND NEIL ARE STILL CHATTING AND JOKING TOGETHER. TRUDY IS ENTHUSIASTICALLY KISSING A COLLEAGUE. BRENT LOOKS OVER ENVIOUSLY. EVENTUALLY HE SIDLES UP AND SITS DOWN NEXT TO TRUDY.

BRENT:
Birthday girl.

TRUDY:
Hello.

BRENT:
Hello. You alright?

TRUDY:
Great.

BRENT:
Yeah. I just want to have a quick word. I've seen you, I know it's your birthday and you're flirting with everyone, you're mucking around, you know, but er, I know you wouldn't take it any further.

TRUDY: (a bit the worse for wear)
Oh, I would!

BRENT:
Would you?

TRUDY:
Yeah!

BRENT:
Well, why not, you know. It's all equal here –

TRUDY:
Well, I'm just having a laugh, aren't I?

BRENT:
I know you are. It's just that I don't know what you're after!

TRUDY:
A man hung like a shire-horse.

BRENT: (embarrassed but soldiering on)
Big, aren't they, big magnificent animals? Say what you mean, don't you? I'm just not sure you're gonna find what you're after.

TRUDY:
See, I'd ask you, but you're a bit old really.

BRENT: (annoyed)
Thirties. Give me a break.

TRUDY:
Born in the thirties, you mean.

BRENT:
You're having a laugh, you're having a laugh. No. I'm thirty something – I'm, I'm ... thirties.

TRUDY:
Yeah, but you've let yourself go a bit, haven't you?

BRENT: (suddenly very angry)
I've let *myself* go a bit? Take a look at yourself. You're an embarrassment, love, to be honest.

HE WALKS AWAY, CROSS.

SCENE 28. INT. OPEN-PLAN OFFICE. DAY.

TIM AND RACHEL ARE TALKING TO BEN AND JAMIE. WE NOTICE THAT, ALMOST UNSEEN, TIM TOUCHES RACHEL'S WAIST AND HER HAND REACHES UP TO TOUCH HIS.

SCENE 29. INT. OPEN-PLAN OFFICE. DAY.

BRENT IS CHATTING TO GARETH AND FINCH. NEIL COMES OVER. THE CORRS' 'DREAMS' IS PLAYING ON THE OFFICE STEREO.

NEIL: (referring to the music)
Who's this?

FINCH:
It's the Corrs isn't it?

NEIL:
Oh, they're alright, the Corrs. They've written some good tunes.

BRENT:
Yeah, they didn't write that one though.

NEIL:
No? Who was that then?

BRENT: (pleased)
Don't you know?

NEIL:
No.

BRENT: (milking it)
Oh, not into pop music, I suppose?

NEIL:
Well, I prefer R'n'B really. So who wrote that?

BRENT:
Fleetwood Mac and I prefer their version as well.

NEIL:
Yeah, well, I know who I'd rather wake up with.

BRENT:
Ooh, sexist, Neil.

FINCH:
They can play my instrument any day.

BRENT:
Oh, bawdy. I don't think you pull women like the Corrs with that sort of attitude, Chris, so ...

FINCH:
Yeah, 'cos you'd know.

BRENT:
Well, I don't know why you're laughing because I'm a dark horse, so you don't –

FINCH:
Yeah, like you could get anyone like the Corrs.

BRENT:
Yeah, what? Well, just 'cos I don't kiss and tell doesn't mean I don't get –

FINCH:
You don't normally kiss, so you've got nothing to tell.

PEOPLE LAUGH, INCLUDING NEIL.

BRENT:
No, no ...

NEIL:
Knowing him, he'd end up with the brother.

PEOPLE LAUGH.

BRENT: (snapping)
No, I wouldn't. No, I wouldn't. No, I'd push the brother out the room, I'd get the other three, and I'd bend 'em all over –

HE MIMES THIS IN ALL ITS GROTESQUE GLORY.

BRENT:
– and I'd do the drummer, the lead singer, and that one who plays the violin.

BRENT MIMES VIOLENTLY SHAGGING THE CORRS. PEOPLE STOP TALKING AND LOOK AT HIM. THERE'S A PAINFUL SILENCE. BRENT REALISES HE'S GONE TOO FAR.

BRENT: (pointing to NEIL)
Oh, see. Your fault, putting filth in people's minds.

THE SILENCE CONTINUES.

CLOSING MUSIC AND END CREDITS, THEN:

PEOPLE ARE MAKING THEIR WAY HOME.

HEADLIGHTS SUDDENLY ILLUMINATE TWO FIGURES CROUCHED BETWEEN A COUPLE OF PARKED CARS.

WE SEE THAT ONE OF THE FIGURES IS CHRIS FINCH, DOING TRUDY FROM BEHIND.

AS QUICKLY AS THEY HAVE APPEARED THEY DISAPPEAR AGAIN AS THE CAR LIGHTS FADE, BUT FAINTLY WE CAN HEAR THEIR VOICES.

TRUDY:
My knees hurt.

FINCH:
Nearly done.

Episode **Four**

CAST
David Brent RICKY GERVAIS
Tim MARTIN FREEMAN
Gareth MACKENZIE CROOK
Dawn LUCY DAVIS
Neil PATRICK BALADI
Rachel STACEY ROCA

with
Lee JOEL BECKETT
Ray TOM GOODMAN-HILL
Jude JENNIFER HENNESEY
Simon MATTHEW HOLNESS
Keith EWEN MACKINTOSH
Speaker 1 CHE GIVEN
Speaker 2 RICHARD WILLS-COTTON

and
Ben Bradshaw, Jamie Deeks, Patrick Driver, Julie Fernandez, Sue Gifford, Rachel Isaac, Jane Lucas, Tony MacMurray, Emma Manton, Alexander Perkins, Philip Pickard and Howard Saddler

SCENE 1. INT. CORRIDOR. DAY.

WE ARE SPYING ON RACHEL AND TIM FROM AFAR. THEY ARE FLIRTING AND TIM KISSES HER NECK. SUDDENLY DAWN APPEARS – TIM AND RACHEL BREAK AWAY EMBARRASSED, AND DAWN REELS, FEELING AWKWARD THAT SHE HAS INTERRUPTED. WE SEE THE SHOCKED LOOK ON HER FACE AS SHE WALKS AWAY.

SCENE 2. INT. RECEPTION. DAY.

OFFICE SCENES. DAWN IS BEHIND RECEPTION. BRENT ARRIVES, WITH JACKET AND BRIEFCASE.

BRENT: (to camera)
Another day, another dollar.
(TO DAWN)
Any mail?

DAWN:
That's your …

DAWN HANDS SOME LETTERS TO HIM AND DOES A DOUBLE-TAKE.

DAWN:
That's an earring.

BRENT:
Whatever. Get over it.

DAWN:
How long have you had that?

BRENT: (playing it cool)
Too long baby.

DAWN:
It's bleeding.

BRENT:
It really stings.

DAWN:
Blimey. Is it an old one that you had to –

BRENT:
Yeah, and I had to push really hard at the time and it was sort of like, it feels like …

DAWN:
But they heal over.

BRENT:
It had healed over. So I think I just, like, opened a sore.

HE FIDDLES WITH THE EARRING.

BRENT:
You know those, um –

TIM AND RACHEL LAUGH OFF-SCREEN. DAWN LOOKS OVER AT THEM.

BRENT:
What you looking at?

DAWN: (defensive)
I'm not looking at anything.

BRENT:
You know those people that came in, Ray and Jude, that I had the meeting with?

DAWN:
I know.

BRENT: (over-explaining, showing off to camera)
Yeah, they do … well, you know, they do sort of training seminars, yeah, and use expert speakers, don't they? They're using me for my … you know …

DAWN:
Expertise?

BRENT:
Yeah. Well, the good news for you, young lady, is you're involved so …

DAWN:
How?

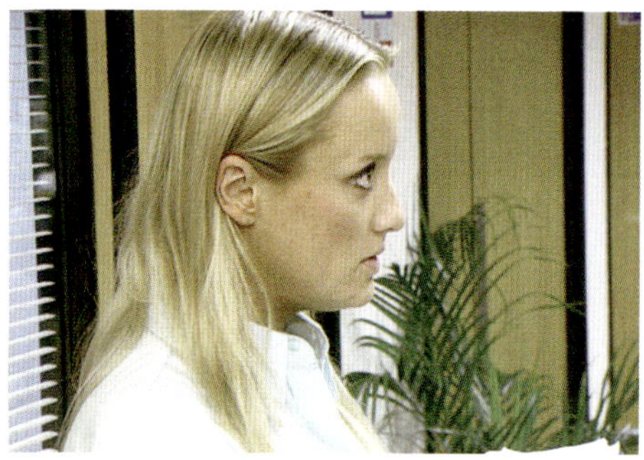

BRENT:
Well, I'm doing one tonight, I'm getting quite a bit of money for it … It's a bit gauche, but three hundred quid – so I need someone just to carry my bag or something, organise …

DAWN:
Oh, well …

BRENT:
Hundred quid. For an hour's work tonight.

DAWN:
Hundred for an hour? That is a lot.

BRENT:
Eighty.

DAWN:
You just said a hundred.

BRENT:
Ninety.

DAWN:
You just said a hundred.

BRENT:
Alright. Get there early then for that 'cos that's sharing the wealth, see? Looking after … that is silly money, a hundred for that. I should've …

SCENE 3. INT. BRENT'S OFFICE. DAY.

BRENT IS SITTING BEHIND HIS DESK.

BRENT:
Very exciting. It's what I … you know … always wanted to do and it's that working … I've had these cards made up.
(READING THEM)
"David Brent. Assertiveness and Guidance Training In Business – If it's in you, I'll find it." 'Cos that's actually what I do, you know. I go along and I just point out what you've already got, I'm like a spiritual guide. The reason I've put "If it's in you, I'll find it" is if I've wasted good time and money looking for it and I can see it's definitely not in you, I don't want to be sued 'cos you haven't got it. So you're not going to get me on that.

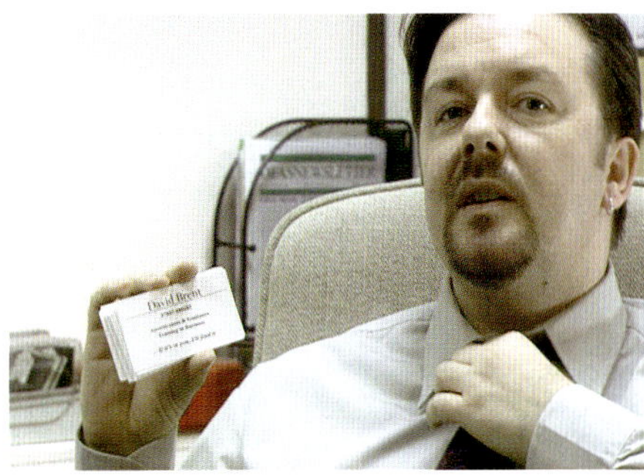

SCENE 4. INT. CORRIDOR. DAY.

TIM AND RACHEL ARE KISSING. GARETH SPOTS THEM.

GARETH:
What's going on here?

TIM:
What does it look like?

GARETH:
How long has this been going on? When were you going to tell me? I can't believe you'd get off with the bird that I fancy.

TIM:
Why can't you believe that, Gareth?

GARETH:
Well, I can't believe there's a bird that fancies you over me for a start. What are you … He's a weird little bloke. Look at his cartoon face and his hair. He looks like a Fisher Price man. And his rubbish clothes. It makes me think there's something wrong with you for a start, but yet in my head I'd still do you, so I'm confused. Alright, I'll ask you straight: is there anything that could happen between us two while this is going on?

RACHEL:
Like what?

GARETH:
What, specifically?

RACHEL:
Yeah.

GARETH:
Hand job? Look, don't answer now. Think about it.

HE LEAVES, HIS FINAL OFFER MADE.

TIM:
Do I look like a Fisher Price man?

RACHEL: (laughing)
Yeah.

TIM:
Do I? What? Don't say yeah …

SCENE 6. INT. OPEN-PLAN OFFICE. DAY.

A MAN IS SITTING AT TIM'S DESK.

DAWN CATCHES TIM AS HE PASSES RECEPTION.

TIM:
Hello.

DAWN:
Your favourite computer geek is here.

TIM:
Jesus.

TIM APPROACHES HIS DESK. SIMON, THE COMPUTER GEEK, IS TAPPING AWAY ON TIM'S KEYBOARD.

TIM:
Alright Simon. How's it going?

TIM DOES A SILENT KARATE CHOP BEHIND SIMON'S BACK.

TIM:
What are you doing with my computer?

SIMON: (smug, pedantic)
Hmm. It's not your computer is it? It's Wernham Hogg's.

TIM:
Right. What are you doing with Wernham Hogg's computer?

SIMON:
You don't need to know.

TIM:
No, I don't need to know, but could you tell me anyway?

SIMON:
I'm installing a firewall.

TIM:
Okay. What's that?

SIMON:
It protects your computer against script kiddies, data collectors, viruses, worms and Trojan horses and it limits your outbound Internet communications. Any more questions?

TIM:
Yes. How long will it take?

SIMON:
Why? Do you want to do it yourself?

TIM:
No. I can't do it myself. How long will it take you, out of interest?

SIMON:
It'll take as long as it takes.

TIM:
Right, um ... How long did it take last time you did this – ?

SIMON: (interrupting)
It's done.

TIM:
Right, thank you.

SIMON:
Now, I'm gonna switch it off. When it comes back on, it'll ask you to hit yes, no or cancel. Hit cancel. Do not hit yes or no.

TIM:
Right.

SIMON:
Did you hear what I said?

TIM:
Yep.

SIMON:
What did I say?

TIM:
Hit cancel.

SIMON:
Good.

TIM:
Thanks.

SCENE 7. INT. BRENT'S OFFICE. DAY.

BRENT IS STILL TALKING TO THE CAMERA.

BRENT:
I'm an educator, I'm a motivator of people, I excite their imaginations, it's like bloody 'Dead Poets Society' sometimes out there. You know, at the end when they all stand on the tables? I wouldn't want them to stand on the tables, literally – it's against health and safety for one thing – but my point is this: life is about communication. We live for three score year and ten and it's –

(HAVING A CONVERSATION WITH HIMSELF)
"Did I communicate?" "Yes, you did." "Did I get something across?" "Yes, you did." "Are you gonna pay me for it?" "Yes, lots." "Thanks very much, not why I do it, but thank you."

SCENE 8. INT. OPEN-PLAN OFFICE. DAY.

SIMON IS WORKING ON GARETH'S COMPUTER. GARETH IS SITTING NEXT TO HIM, WATCHING HIM TAP AWAY. TIM IS AT HIS DESK, FORCED TO LISTEN TO THEIR INANE CHATTER.

GARETH:
Going go-karting again at the weekend with the lads.

SIMON:
Oh yeah, what, down SuperKarts?

GARETH:
Yeah.

SIMON:
You any good?

GARETH:
Came first last time I went. Eight minutes, fifty-one. Got a certificate.

HE POINTS TO A CERTIFICATE STUCK UP NEAR HIS DESK.

SIMON:
Yeah, well, I went down there the first day it opened, right? I did a couple of laps; I pulled over; the bloke that runs the thing came over and said, “Oi. No professionals.” I took my helmet off. I said, “I’m not a professional”. He said, “You’re not a professional?” I said, “No.” He said, “Well, you should be. If I was you I’d take up Formula One, and if you drive like that you’ll probably be the best in the country.” I said, “I’m not interested, I’m making shitloads out of computers.”

GARETH:
Have you ever had a go at speedway?

SIMON:
Have you?

GARETH:
Yeah.

SIMON:
Right, well, I was doing it once, and erm, I was bombing it round and some idiot had left, like, a ramp thing out –

TIM:
Litter bugs.

SIMON:
– I could see the people were going, “Oh my God, if that guy hits that ramp going at that speed, he’s definitely dead.” I hit the ramp, I took off in the air, I turned over in the air, and they were going, “Well, he’s definitely dead now.” I landed on my wheels, pulled over and said, “What were you worried about?”

TIM REACTS.

SCENE 9. INT. RECEPTION. DAY.

NEIL IS TALKING TO DAWN. BRENT WANDERS PAST.

BRENT:
What's this then, a mother's meeting?

NEIL:
David, Dawn tells me you're shutting down reception at five.

BRENT:
Well, just half an hour early today.

NEIL:
Do you think it can run okay without her?

BRENT:
Yeah, phones'll go straight ... They can answer their own phones. They can do their own post tonight, just once.

NEIL:
Well, that's good, so we can probably lose her altogether then, can we?

BRENT:
What do you mean?

NEIL:
Well, if you don't need a receptionist, we may as well let her go. Either she's needed or she's not.

BRENT:
We do need a receptionist.

NEIL:
Well, my point is, David, you haven't put a system in place, you know. For your own needs you've told Dawn to shut down reception at five, you haven't told these people they can pick up the phone if it rings. I mean, does Dawn know that they can do their own post?

BRENT: (to DAWN)
Dawn, they can do their own post tonight.

DAWN:
Okay.

NEIL:
It's no use telling her now.

BRENT:
Well …

NEIL:
It's just there's no system in place … You're not thinking things through.
(FRUSTRATED)
I'm tired of this fuzzy thinking, David.

BRENT:
Alright, chill out, don't have a cow, mate.

NEIL:
Don't talk to me like you've forgotten who's in charge here. Let me remind you, I'm your boss, okay?

BRENT:
Yes.

NEIL:
Just try and think things through.

NEIL WALKS OFF.

BRENT LOOKS AT THE CAMERA, THEN AT DAWN.

BRENT: (to DAWN)
That was your fault again. I took the rap for you, didn't I? You …

HE WALKS OFF, ANNOYED.

SCENE 10. INT. OPEN-PLAN OFFICE. DAY.

SIMON AND GARETH ARE IN DISCUSSION. TIM IS LISTENING AND REACTING.

SIMON:
Once, right, when Bruce Lee was filming, one of the extras just came over and just started a fight …

GARETH:
Oh yeah, I know this, he was amazing at Kung Fu, but Bruce Lee just did a round-house on him …

SIMON:
Well, no: he smashed him through a wall. And instead of firing him he just said, "Go back to where you were, let's get on with the film."

TIM:
Man, those cats were as fast as lightning.

GARETH:
You know when he was fighting Chuck Norris in 'Enter the Dragon'?

SIMON:
No.

GARETH:
You not seen that?

SIMON:
No.

GARETH:
Have you not … I can't … That is a classic.

SIMON:
No, I've not seen him fight Chuck Norris in 'Enter the Dragon', I've seen him fight Chuck Norris in 'Way of the Dragon'.

GARETH:
Oh, that's what I meant, that's what I meant.

SIMON:
Oh, is it?

<u>GARETH:</u>
Yeah.

<u>SIMON:</u>
Why did you say you'd seen him fight Chuck Norris in 'Enter the Dragon'? He fights Bob Wall in both, but Norris is only in 'Way of the Dragon'.

<u>GARETH:</u>
Yeah, I know, so when he was fighting Chuck Norris –

<u>SIMON:</u>
In what?

<u>GARETH:</u>
In 'Way of the Dragon' –

<u>SIMON:</u>
Correct. At last.

HE THROWS A LOOK AT THE CAMERA, AS IF TO SAY "SEE HOW I JUST CAUGHT THIS GUY OUT?"

<u>SIMON:</u>
You know Bruce Lee's not really dead, don't you? Yeah, it's in a book. What he did was he faked his own death so that he could work undercover for the Hong Kong police, infiltrating drugs gangs and the Triads.

RACHEL WANDERS OVER AND SITS ON TIM'S DESK.

<u>GARETH:</u>
Yeah, I reckon that's true.

<u>TIM:</u>
Yeah, I reckon that's true, 'cos if you were gonna send someone undercover to investigate the Triads you'd probably want the world's most famous Chinese film star.

RACHEL LAUGHS AT TIM'S COMMENTS. SIMON IS ANNOYED.

<u>SIMON:</u> (to TIM, nasty)
Oh. Gone off Dawn now, have you?

<u>RACHEL:</u>
What?

TIM:
What? What are you talking about? Just shut up, shut up.

SCENE 11. INT. RECEPTION. DAY.

OFFICE SCENES.

LEE AND DAWN ARE CHATTING. TIM WALKS PAST.

LEE:
Oi Tim, you shagged her yet or what?

TIM:
What?

LEE:
Your bird? What's her name?

DAWN:
Rachel.

LEE:
Yeah, Rachel. Have you done her yet or what?

DAWN:
Of course he hasn't.

SHE WAITS FOR CONFIRMATION OF THIS FROM TIM.

TIM:
I don't kiss and tell, Lee.

LEE:
I bet you bloody have, haven't you?

DAWN IS WAITING FOR THE ANSWER, BUT TRYING TO LOOK UNINTERESTED. THE ANSWER SHE'S WAITING FOR DOESN'T COME.

TIM:
Lips are sealed. Don't ask me.

TIM JOKES THIS OFF AND WALKS AWAY. LEE WATCHES RACHEL CHATTING TO AN EMPLOYEE.

LEE:
No, he's done well there.

DAWN:
What do you mean, done well?

LEE:
She's tasty. She's nice.

DAWN:
But you don't even know her.

LEE:
No, I mean she's very attractive.

DAWN:
She's not very attractive.

SCENE 12. INT. BRENT'S OFFICE. DAY.

GARETH IS HELPING BRENT REHEARSE HIS SPEECH.

BRENT:
I think Ray'll introduce me and I'll come out, and I'll do a bit of, you know, a few gags and then I'll go –
(READING FROM NOTES)
"Right, you have to be thick-skinned in business. It doesn't matter if you're the tea boy or the general manager, people will try and rock your confidence and shake your spirit. Do not listen to them, yeah? Let's try a little exercise." Then I'll just go into the audience and I'll pick on someone at random, I'll just go, er …
(POINTING TO GARETH)
You sir. What's your name?

GARETH STARES AT HIM.

BRENT:
Say your name.

GARETH:
Leroy.

BRENT:
Where's Leroy come from?

GARETH:
The coloured fella off of 'Fame'.

BRENT:
Well, use your own name.

GARETH:
Oh, Gareth.

BRENT:
Hi Gareth. Gareth – insult me, yeah? Let me show you that sticks and stones may break my bones, but names will never hurt me … Just throw some insults at me and I'll show you how to roll with the punches.

GARETH:
Um … The Swindon lot don't seem to respect you.

BRENT: (annoyed)
Why would they say that, they don't know me, they're not going to know that … and it's not true. Do something else.

GARETH:
Um.
(THINKS)
A lot of people are laughing at the heels on your shoes.

BRENT: (angry)
I'm not gonna be wearing the shoes, am I?

GARETH:
Are you going to be wearing the earring?

BRENT:
What, they're having a go at that as well, are they?

GARETH:
Some people are.

BRENT:
What else?

GARETH:
Um, they've given you a nickname.

BRENT:
What, the Swindon lot?

GARETH:
Yeah, but everyone's using it.

BRENT:
What is it?

GARETH:
Well, I don't really ...

BRENT:
No, come on, what is it?

GARETH:
Bluto.

BRENT:
The villain from 'Popeye'?

GARETH:
Yeah.

BRENT:
What, is it because of the beard?

GARETH:
No, it's 'cos he's –

HE PUFFS OUT HIS FACE AND CHEST TO SIGNIFY 'A FAT BLOKE'.

BRENT:
What's that? That's ... I can't believe this.

BRENT WALKS TOWARDS THE DOOR.

<u>GARETH:</u>
Don't go out. They'll know it was me that told you.
(WHINEY)
David.

BRENT IGNORES HIS PLEA AND GOES OUT ANYWAY.

SCENE 13. INT. OPEN-PLAN OFFICE. DAY.

<u>BRENT:</u> (addressing the room)
Hello, sorry everybody. Um, look, we are one big happy family here, yeah? Now, I've been trying to welcome you new guys, you know, I didn't want you here, but you're here now, so, you know, well done, welcome. But if there's one thing I don't like it's nicknames, yeah? Because nicknames are … bad … names, yeah? They're not helpful, yeah? They can be very hurtful to … Not to me – it's like water off a duck's back – but, you know, to –

<u>EMPLOYEE:</u>
You used to call Malcolm Kojak.

<u>BRENT:</u>
That was affectionate. He was a great detective, and a fine actor.

<u>EMPLOYEE:</u>
Well, maybe Mr Toad's affectionate.

<u>BRENT:</u>
Who's Mr Toad?

<u>GARETH:</u>
Some people call you that as well.

<u>BRENT:</u>
I thought I was Bluto?

<u>GARETH:</u>
Yeah, Bluto and Mr Toad.

BRENT: (to EMPLOYEE)
Why am I Mr Toad?

THE EMPLOYEE PUFFS OUT HIS FACE AND CHEST EXACTLY AS GARETH DID.

BRENT: (taken aback)
There's the face again. What? It's an insult, isn't it? Very … Body fascism, that's what that is. The toad is the ugliest of all the amphibians. I can't … If we're handing out insults for being fat, let's have a go at him.

HE POINTS AT BIG KEITH.

BRENT:
Look at him. And he's got glasses: four eyes as well. Why don't we call him Fatty Fatty Toad Boy? If we're … At least start on him and then move on. Mr Toad! I can't …

HE WALKS BACK INTO HIS OFFICE, STILL STUNNED.

SCENE 14. INT. OPEN-PLAN OFFICE. DAY.

NEIL IS CHATTING WITH SOME OF THE SWINDON STAFF.

NEIL:
Everything adding up alright?

OLIVER:
Yeah, just about. It was a real mess beforehand.

NEIL:
Was it? But you're on top of it now?

OLIVER:
Yeah, it's alright.

NEIL:
What about you, Brenda, how are things?

BRENDA:
Yeah, alright, but I didn't get my wages through again.

NEIL:
Did you not? Really?

BRENDA:
Uhuh.

NEIL:
Did you tell David?

BRENDA:
Yeah, I told him in time.

NEIL:
Oh, I'm really sorry about that. Let me … It's sorted. Let me sort that out for you now.

BRENDA:
I don't want to cause any –

NEIL:
No, don't worry, it's fine.

WE FOLLOW NEIL AS HE WALKS TOWARDS BRENT'S OFFICE. HE OPENS THE DOOR TO FIND GARETH KNEELING ON THE FLOOR, HOLDING BRENT'S LEGS, AS BRENT DOES SOME STOMACH CRUNCHES.

BRENT REACTS, EMBARRASSED, OUT OF BREATH.

THEY BOTH GET UP.

NEIL:
Working hard?

BRENT:
Working out. Fit body, fit mind.

NEIL:
Good. A couple of things –

GARETH IS DOING HIS COOLING-DOWN EXERCISES. NEIL STARES AT HIM IMPATIENTLY, SO GARETH DECIDES NOW IS PERHAPS NOT THE TIME.

NEIL:
A couple of things, David – did your wages go through okay this month?

BRENT:
Yeah.

NEIL:
Yours, Gareth?

GARETH:
Yep. Fine.

NEIL:
Good, so you two are okay. Phew. Why then has one of your team come to me saying they haven't been paid this month?

BRENT GROANS, GRINNING, CLEARLY STALLING, SEARCHING FOR AN ANSWER.

BRENT:
Oh. No.

NEIL WAITS TO HEAR THE EXCUSE.

BRENT TALKING HEAD. INT. DAY.

BRENT:
He fears my methods because he doesn't understand my methods, you know. Human nature, the unknown, sure, but relax, you know? I don't want all this
(AS NEIL)
"Oh, er, what you doing, what you doing? How are you doing it?"
(AS HIMSELF)
"No. Judge me by my results."

SCENE 15. INT. BRENT'S OFFICE. DAY.

NEIL AND BRENT ARE IN THE MIDDLE OF AN INCREASINGLY HEATED DEBATE. GARETH LOOKS ON.

NEIL:
This is not the first time you've forgotten something important. It's not the first time this week, and it worries me when someone feels they have to go over your head and come to me.

BRENT:
Snitches.

NEIL:
Do you know I've never seen you write anything down. You've got two computers, I don't even know what you use them for. You've got to have some sort of system.

BRENT: (tapping his head)
It's all up there.

NEIL:
Yeah, but it's not all up there, is it?

BRENT:
Most of it is.

NEIL:
Look David, I'll tell you now: when I was managing the Swindon branch, our perception of your branch was: "They're having a laugh."

BRENT:
Thanks very much.

NEIL:
No, no, not in a good way. Having a laugh, mucking around at the expense of Wernham Hogg.

BRENT:
Well, who's to say if they weren't mucking around, having a laugh all the time, it wouldn't be much worse?

NEIL:
I'm not interested in that, David. Look, I get the impression that you'd rather be popular than steer the ship in the right direction.

BRENT:
Well, rubbish. And I resent the accusation, because this branch has performed very well, so –

NEIL:
– Well, it's performed okay. I want it to perform a lot better.

BRENT:
There you go. What is better? Because I could show you a graph of people versus task and where does the line go –

NEIL:
– The line goes where I want it to go. Now, if you can't improve your margin and your volume sales, with or without making people laugh, if you can't do that, you and I are going to have to have a very serious chat.

BRENT:
Is this why you're around all the time? Keeping tabs on me? Because I don't need a babysitter.

NEIL:
Well, with respect David, I think you do. You know, I'm aware of this management training thing you're doing tonight and I'm worried it's going to affect your performance at work.

BRENT:
That's extra-curricular, you know, some people play golf.

NEIL:
Well, I play golf.

BRENT:
There you go, so …

NEIL:
Yes, but I'm performing as I want me to perform. You're not performing as I want you to perform.

BRENT:
I'm performing as I want me to perform.

NEIL:
I don't want you to perform like that.

BRENT:
It's a good performance. Let's agree to disagree.

NEIL:
No, let's agree that you agree with me.

BRENT:
Ooh, you're hard. Showing off 'cos …

BRENT POINTS AT THE CAMERA, LOOKING FOR SUPPORT.

NEIL:
Well, I think I've made my point, David. Okay, I'll see you later.

NEIL LEAVES.

BRENT AND GARETH SIT IN SILENCE FOR A MOMENT. GARETH, UNSOLICITED, DECIDES IT WOULD BE A GOOD MOMENT TO START MASSAGING BRENT'S NECK. BRENT IS LOST IN THOUGHT AND DOESN'T NOTICE STRAIGHT AWAY. SUDDENLY, HE REALISES WHAT GARETH IS DOING.

BRENT:
What you doing?

GARETH:
You looked a bit tense.

<u>BRENT:</u>
I am. With him …

<u>GARETH:</u> (massaging BRENT's neck)
Doesn't that feel nice?

<u>BRENT:</u>
Yeah, but –

BRENT POINTS TO CAMERA, AS IF TO SAY, "WHAT ABOUT THEM?"

<u>GARETH:</u>
Shall we do some more work on your abs?

<u>BRENT:</u>
Not now.

GARETH STARTS DOING A LIGHT CHOPPING ACTION ON BRENT'S SHOULDERS. BRENT STARES BLANKLY AT THE CAMERA.

<u>SCENE 16. INT. OPEN-PLAN OFFICE/RECEPTION. DAY.</u>

OFFICE SCENES.

DAWN HAS HER COAT ON AND IS GLANCING TOWARDS TIM, WHO IS WORKING. EVENTUALLY SHE WALKS OVER AND HOVERS BEHIND HIS DESK UNTIL HE NOTICES HER.

<u>DAWN:</u> (looking toward BRENT's office)
Is he ready yet?

<u>TIM:</u>
Who?

DAWN:
David.

TIM:
Oh, right. I don't know.

DAWN:
So what you doing tonight?

TIM:
I think we're just gonna go out to the pub.

DAWN:
"We" is – ?

TIM:
Me and Rachel.

DAWN:
Excellent. Just a couple of pints?

TIM:
Couple of pints.

DAWN:
Well, think of me, stuck with …
(SHE GESTURES TOWARDS BRENT'S OFFICE)
Ooh, you should come, for a laugh.

TIM:
I think we'd better stay out of it.

DAWN:
Yep. Definitely. Wise. Alright babes.

TIM:
Alright mate.

DAWN:
I'll see you.

TIM:
Have a good night. See you later.

SHE TOUCHES HIM ON THE ARM AND MANAGES TO FIND A WAY TO HOLD HIS HAND FOR A MOMENT AS SHE MOVES AWAY. TIM NOTICES THIS AND CONSIDERS IT FOR A MOMENT, BUT HIS THOUGHTS ARE INTERRUPTED BY BRENT STRIDING INTO VIEW FROM HIS OFFICE. DAWN, IN FRONT OF HIM, IS MAKING A FACE OF SHEER DISBELIEF. BRENT IS CARRYING A HOLDALL AND HAS CHANGED CLOTHES. HE'S GONE FOR THE 'LOVEJOY' LOOK – WHITE T-SHIRT TUCKED INTO PALE BLUE WRANGLERS, BIG WHITE TRAINERS, AND HIS LEATHER JACKET – PLUS A BASEBALL CAP.

<u>BRENT:</u> (to TIM)
See you later. Wish us luck on our date. It's not a date is it? She's got a boyfriend. And I'm paying her! What sort of date would that be? I think you know. And a hundred quid: what would I get for that? Not that I would, 'cos you wouldn't, I mean, but … Everything, I imagine … I'm not imagining any of it, but I do know what sort of … I'm just …

HE DECIDES TO GET OUT WHILE HE STILL CAN.

<u>BRENT:</u>
Okay, then, there we go. I'm just … Carry that, that's what you're being paid for.

BRENT THROWS THE HUGE HOLDALL ON THE FLOOR AND DAWN HEAVES IT OVER HER SHOULDERS.

<u>SCENE 17. INT. COMMUNITY CENTRE CORRIDOR. NIGHT.</u>

BRENT IS ARRIVING WITH RAY AND JUDE. THEY STRIDE DOWN THE CORRIDOR WHILE RAY EXPLAINS THINGS, LEAVING THE DOOR TO SWING SHUT ON DAWN, STILL CARRYING THE ENORMOUS HOLDALL.

<u>SCENE 18. INT. COMMUNITY CENTRE HALL. NIGHT.</u>

PEOPLE ARE TAKING THEIR SEATS.

SCENE 19. INT. COMMUNITY CENTRE BACKSTAGE AREA. NIGHT.

BRENT IS HOPPING AROUND, LIKE A BOXER BEFORE A FIGHT.

RAY:
The other three guys, they've all done it before, so … I'll introduce you when they get here.

BRENT:
I love being backstage …

RAY:
Can we just take a photo, it's for the website and the newsletter, if that's okay?

BRENT:
No problem. You got to take a light reading?

RAY IS HOLDING A VERY BASIC DISPOSABLE CAMERA.

RAY:
I think we'll be okay. If you just …

BRENT:
Yeah.

BRENT STRIKES A POSE THAT WOULD LOOK SUITABLE ONLY IF HE WERE A POP SINGER ON THE COVER OF *SMASH HITS*.

RAY:
I mean just be yourself, you know. A bit more relaxed?

THE CAMERA IS OFF BRENT. WHEN IT PANS BACK, HE'S LYING FACE DOWN ON THE TABLE, PROPPING HIS HEAD UP WITH HIS HANDS, LIKE A 1950S MOVIE STARLET, ONE FOOT LOLLING COQUETTISHLY.

BRENT:
Something like that?

RAY:
Not quite.

BRENT:
Okay.

HE RECLINES ON THE TABLE, KNEE BENT, LEANING ON HIS ELBOW.

RAY:
Maybe if you just sit down.

BRENT:
You're the boss.

BRENT GRABS A CHAIR, AND SWINGS IT UNDER HIS LEGS SO THAT HE'S SITTING ON IT BACKWARDS. HE DOES A 'VOGUE'-STYLE POSE.

RAY RELUCTANTLY TAKES A PICTURE. JUDE WATCHES IN DISBELIEF.

SCENE 20. INT. COMMUNITY CENTRE CORRIDOR. NIGHT.

THE OTHER SPEAKERS, DRESSED IN SUITS, ARE STANDING CHATTING. ONE OF THEM IS SMOKING. BRENT APPROACHES THEM.

BRENT:
Alright? Are you guys talking at this gig as well?

SPEAKER #1:
Yeah. Just having a sneaky joint.

BRENT LOOKS EDGY AT THE MENTION OF DRUGS, BUT TRIES TO PLAY IT COOL.

<u>BRENT:</u>
Partially decriminalised now anyway, isn't it? So – at last. Go for it!
(ACTING STREETWISE)
What is it, skunk?

<u>SPEAKER #1:</u>
No, it's just weed. Do you want a little taste?

<u>BRENT:</u>
No.

<u>SPEAKER #1:</u>
Are you sure?

<u>BRENT:</u>
Yeah. No. I'm on a diet and when I get wasted I go to munchies-city so ... you know.

THE OTHER SPEAKERS SMIRK.

<u>BRENT:</u>
I'm mad enough without the gear as well so er, I'll take a raincheck – I'll catch you later, yeah?

<u>SPEAKER #1:</u>
Yeah.

<u>BRENT:</u>
Chill.

HE SKULKS OFF, TRYING TO LOOK HIP.

SCENE 21. INT. COMMUNITY CENTRE HALL. NIGHT.

RAY IS ADDRESSING THE AUDIENCE.

RAY:
Well, we've got four speakers for you tonight so no messing about. To begin with, from Sound Investments, Mr Mark Found.

SPEAKER #1:
Let me dispel a myth: just because you're a success in your life, some people will tell you that you shouldn't be able to sleep at night. You should. Why? Because this is a business.

FADE OUT.

SCENE 22. INT. COMMUNITY CENTRE HALL. NIGHT.

THE SECOND SPEAKER IS COMING TO THE END OF HIS SPEECH.

SPEAKER #2:
Your future hasn't happened yet. You shape it. You're in the driving seat. Thanks.

RAY:
Thanks to Richard Clark there from Stockport Graphics. Now with some words of advice on motivational techniques, from Wernham Hogg, Mr David Brent.

BRENT GETS UP AND SAUNTERS TO THE FRONT. HE RIPS OFF HIS BASEBALL CAP AND, WITHOUT LOOKING, FLINGS IT TOWARDS DAWN. IT SMACKS HER IN THE FACE.

HE PROWLS AROUND THE STAGE, STARING AT THE AUDIENCE, THEN THROWS OPEN THE EXIT DOOR.

BRENT: (dramatic)
Get out!

PEOPLE STARE AT HIM IN SILENCE.

BRENT:
Go on! I've opened the door for you, yeah? If you don't want to make it, go now. Yeah? Save us all a bit of time, yeah, if you don't think you can cut it. No? Good.

HE GOES TO CLOSE THE DOOR. A CLEANER APPEARS JUST AS HE'S ABOUT TO CLOSE IT.

CLEANER: (ruining the moment)
Have you finished in here?

BRENT:
No. I'm in a ...

HE RETURNS TO HIS AUDIENCE, PUT OFF MOMENTARILY.

BRENT:
Okay ... You're all looking at me, and you're going, "Well, yeah, you're a success, you've achieved your goals, you're reaping the rewards. Sure, but, oi Brent! Is all you care about chasing the Yankee dollar?" Let me show you something I always keep with me.

BRENT GETS OUT A LITTLE POCKET-SIZED BOOK.

BRENT:
Just a little book.
(READING THE COVER)
'Collected Meditations'. It's a collection of philosophers, writers, thinkers, Native American wisdom, which I ... And it's really showing you that the spiritual side needs as much care and attention as the physical side. It's about feeding the soul, yeah? Evolving spirituality – foreword by Duncan Goodhew, so ... Can I read one which I think –
(READING)
"If all men were to bring their miseries together in one place most would be glad to take each his own home again rather than take a portion out of the common stock."

(TO AUDIENCE)
It's saying for the first time, you know, the grass isn't always greener on the other side. Don't look over your neighbour's fence and go, "Ooh, he's got a better car than me, ooh, he's got a more attractive wife." We all wake up and we go, "Oh, I ache, I'm not eighteen any more, you know, I'm thirty n– … I'm … I'm in my thirties." But so what? "At least I've got my health." And if you haven't got your health, if you've got one leg, "At least I haven't got two legs missing." And if you have lost both legs and both arms, just go, "At least I'm not dead". I'd rather be dead in that situation, to be honest. I'm not saying people like that should be, you know, put down.

HE SUBCONSCIOUSLY MIMES SOMEONE BEING 'PUT DOWN' BY LETHAL INJECTION. THE AUDIENCE STARES AT HIM, STONY-FACED.

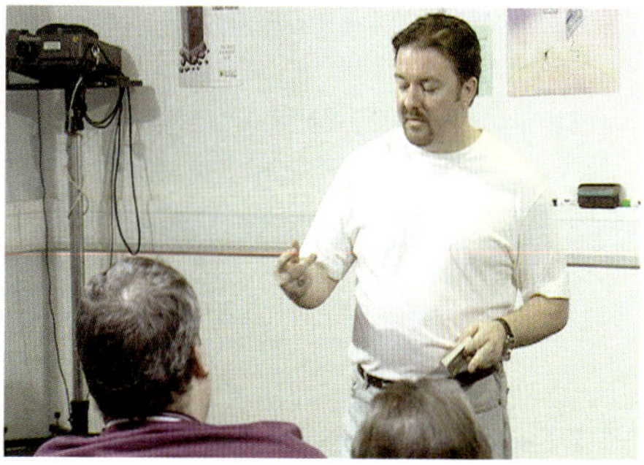

<u>BRENT:</u>
I'm saying that in my life I'd rather not live without arms and legs, because … I'm just getting into yoga, for one thing, so, in my opinion …

FADE OUT ON RAY AND JUDE LOOKING UTTERLY BEWILDERED.

SCENE 23. INT. COMMUNITY CENTRE HALL. NIGHT.

BRENT IS STILL CENTRESTAGE.

BRENT:
Are you familiar with the term "laughter is the best medicine"? Well, it's true. When you laugh, your brain releases endorphins, yeah? Your stress hormones are reduced, and the oxygen supply to your blood is increased, so you feel … I try and laugh several times a day. Just because it makes you feel good, so let's try that.
(HE LAUGHS)
Hey, just … Come on, trust me, you'll feel …

HE THROWS BACK HIS HEAD AND LAUGHS SOME MORE. NO-ONE JOINS IN. HE BEGINS WITH A FEW TITTERS, AND WORKS HIS WAY VIA SOME CHUCKLES TO SOME MIGHTY GUFFAWS. DAWN CAN'T BELIEVE WHAT SHE'S SEEING. HER TALKING HEAD BEGINS OVER THIS.

DAWN TALKING HEAD. INT. DAY.

DAWN:
I'd be lying if I said my life had turned out exactly as I'd expected. My old school just recently had a school reunion, which I didn't go to, but one girl in my class it turns out, right, that she is now running her own Internet auction website, making a fortune, and is happily married to a marine biologist.
(PAUSE)
She used to eat chalk!

SCENE 24. INT. COMMUNITY CENTRE HALL. NIGHT.

BRENT IS WINDING UP.

BRENT:
Okay, well that's about it from yours truly. Thanks for taking all I had to throw at you. I'm spent, but I am now going to make like a banana, and split!

NO-ONE LAUGHS. HE POINTS AT AN AUDIENCE MEMBER.

BRENT:
He got it. Okay, before I go though, promise me you'll remember one thing. Yeah? Just remember –

HE PUTS ON A TAPE. TINA TURNER'S 'THE BEST' BURSTS ON AND BRENT LEAPS UP ONTO THE STAGE, JIGGING AROUND AND SINGING. IT IS HIDEOUSLY INAPPROPRIATE.

BRENT:
Yes!

TINA TURNER CONTINUES AT FULL VOLUME.

BRENT:
Come on, listen to her, listen to her!

THE AUDIENCE LOOKS NONPLUSSED. BRENT IS SINGING ALONG ENTHUSIASTICALLY.

BRENT:
Come on, get into it!

BRENT IS STILL CLAPPING AND JUMPING AROUND.

BRENT:
I've been David Brent, you've been "The Best". See you later.

HE RUNS OUT OF THE DOOR AT THE SIDE OF THE STAGE. TINA CONTINUES BELTING OUT 'THE BEST'. NO ONE QUITE KNOWS WHAT THEY'VE JUST SEEN. JUDE EVENTUALLY GETS UP AND SWITCHES OFF THE DEAFENING SOUND.

JUDE:
Um, yes, our thanks to David –

BRENT POPS HIS HEAD BACK ROUND THE OPEN DOOR.

BRENT: (annoyed)
Who stopped it?

JUDE:
I did.

BRENT:
No, don't stop it. Leave it going right to the end, 'til I get … Don't do that again next time, okay?

JUDE:
Sorry.

BRENT OFFERS A FINAL TRIUMPHANT SALUTE TO HIS AUDIENCE AND SKIPS OFF AGAIN.

JUDE:
David Brent from Wernham Hogg.

SCENE 25. INT. COMMUNITY CENTRE BACKSTAGE. NIGHT.

BRENT IS HOPPING AROUND EXCITEDLY, ADRENALIN PUMPING. DAWN IS TRYING TO BE VAGUELY SUPPORTIVE.

BRENT:
I'll let you into a little secret now, right? Before I went out there I was worried whether I still had it. I'll let you be the judge of that. High five! Don't leave me hanging, Dawn.

SHE GIVES HIM FIVE.

BRENT:
Oh God. Oh Jesus. Oh, here he is …

RAY COMES IN.

BRENT TAKES OFF HIS SHIRT AND THROWS HIS DIRTY T-SHIRT AT DAWN. SHE PUTS IT DOWN HURRIEDLY.

BRENT: (to RAY)
Tina a bit too much for you?

RAY:
Possibly.

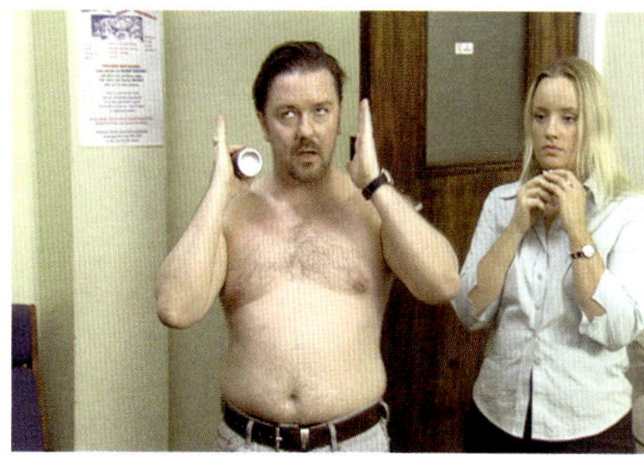

BRENT:
Oh, that's your job. Hold me back, 'cause when I'm out there – I am … Whoooooooeeeee! – And it's like –
(HE MAKES APPROPRIATE SWEEPING HAND GESTURES)
– So, that's up to you I'm afraid. Oh gee.

HE PULLS A DEODORANT OUT OF HIS BAG AND SPRAYS IT WILDLY OVER HIMSELF AND DAWN.

BRENT:
Tell you what though, they seemed to go for it, didn't they?

RAY IS NON-COMMITTAL. JUDE COMES IN.

JUDE:
Knock knock.

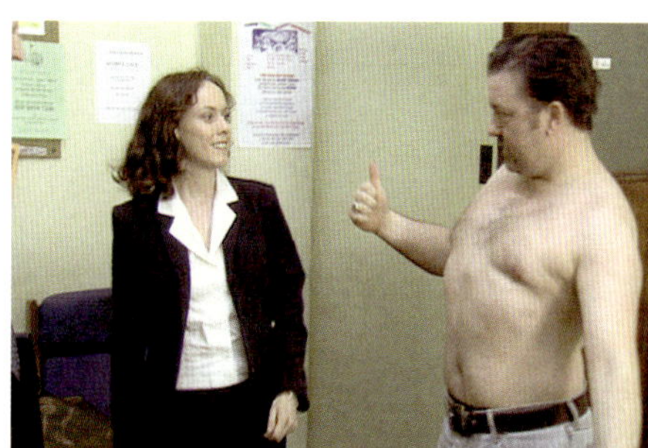

WITH HIS SHIRT OFF, BRENT PULLS IN HIS STOMACH.

BRENT:
Hiya. You alright?

JUDE:
Yeah … Well done …

BRENT:
What d'you think?

JUDE:
Well, my tastes are quite traditional.

BRENT:
Bit too rock 'n' roll for you?

JUDE:
Possibly.

BRENT:
Each his own. Each his own. Better warn you now. That was me on a seven. So wait till you see me on a nine or ten.
(TO DAWN)
Innit?

RAY HANDS HIM A CHEQUE.

RAY:
There's your cheque.

BRENT:
Thanking you. Well, there you go.
(GIGGLING EXCITEDLY)
More importantly though, what pub are we going to? More important than that – three hundred quid! I don't think so. Where we going?

BRENT IS HOPPING AROUND, PUNCHING THE AIR AGAIN.

RAY:
We can't, we're just gonna grab some food, go home.

BRENT:
Pizza, yeah? Never mind Pizza Express, what about "beer express" first? "Next stop, drunkenness." It doesn't have to be. Go anywhere you want. Chinese, Indian, as long as it's, you know … It's on me. Here we go, the three musketeers.

THEY EXIT AND WE HEAR THEIR VOICES FROM THE CORRIDOR. DAWN IS LEFT BEHIND TO CLEAR UP ALL BRENT'S BAGS AND PROPS.

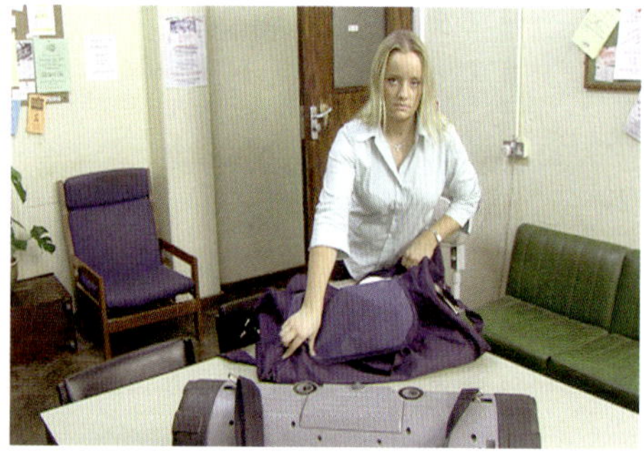

JUDE:
Oh, I just remembered, I can't …

RAY: (not wanting to be left with BRENT)
What d'you mean?

JUDE:
I just … remembered something I've got to do.

BRENT:
Uh oh. Just us two, then. Oh, no! What sort of clubs are round here?

RAY:
I'm not going to a club.

BRENT:
You bloody are.

CLOSING MUSIC AND END CREDITS, THEN:

DAWN FINALLY LEAVES, BURDENED WITH BRENT'S BAGS.

Episode **Five**

CAST
David Brent RICKY GERVAIS
Tim MARTIN FREEMAN
Gareth MACKENZIE CROOK
Dawn LUCY DAVIS
Neil PATRICK BALADI
Rachel STACEY ROCA
Chris Finch RALPH INESON

with
Jennifer STIRLING GALLACHER
Lee JOEL BECKETT
Keith EWEN MACINTOSH
Photographer HUGH PARKER
Jimmy the Perv BRUCE MACKINNON
The Oggmonster STEPHEN MERCHANT

and
Ben Bradshaw, Jamie Deeks, Patrick Driver, Julie Fernandez, Rachel Isaac, Jane Lucas, Tony MacMurray, Emma Manton, Alexander Perkins, Philip Pickard and Howard Saddler

SCENE 1. INT. RECEPTION AREA. DAY.

DAWN IS BEHIND THE RECEPTION DESK, WATCHING BRENT AS HE ADDRESSES THE CAMERA.

WE HAVE NEVER SEEN BRENT AS GLEEFUL AS HE IS TODAY. HE CANNOT STOP GIGGLING. HE'S LIKE A CHILD AT CHRISTMAS.

BRENT: (giggling)
Hello, just another normal day at the office, innit?

BRENT TURNS HIS BACK ON THE CAMERA. WHEN HE TURNS BACK HE'S WEARING A PLASTIC RED NOSE.

BRENT:
Just a normal day, innit, so … What?
(TO DAWN)
What are you laughing at?

SHE IS NOT LAUGHING.

BRENT: (giggling)
No, obviously Red Nose day – it's always a good laugh, we had a …

HE SPOTS SOMETHING OFF-SCREEN.

BRENT:
Keith, here, right. This is the sort of thing …

BIG KEITH APPEARS. HE IS DRESSED AS ALI G.

BRENT: (giggling)
Ali G. Ali Keith.
(HE SPOTS SOMETHING ELSE)
Gareth come here, right –
(TO CAMERA)
Look at this, normal day, right? Just a normal office.

WE SEE GARETH HOPPING OVER.

BRENT: (laughing hysterically)
What are you doing?

GARETH:
I've got to hop everywhere. I'm being sponsored.

BRENT: (to camera)
Hopping everywhere! So that's the sort of thing we'll be doing today. We always have a good laugh; raised quite a lot last time, didn't we?
(HE SUDDENLY BECOMES OVER-EARNEST)
But you know, on a serious note, it is Comic Relief and we are raising money for people who are starving to death. If I make people laugh while I'm saving lives, sue me. But, er, you know …
(HE NOTICES KEITH AND GIGGLES AGAIN)
Do it.

KEITH: (with usual lack of emotion)
Booyakasha.

BRENT:
That's an accountant. And that's the boss encouraging it. So what sort of a day is it? Is it normal? I've got the Slough Gazette coming down to take a photo.

GARETH:
What time are they coming down?

BRENT:
About five-ish. So …

GARETH:
They'll love us, won't they?

BRENT:
No, I think it's just me. I've got something planned, so …

GARETH:
But we can all be in it though?

BRENT:
Well, not really, I called them, so …

GARETH:
But they'll love us, all being stupid –

BRENT: (annoyed)
Stop trying to worm your way into someone else's photo.

HE TAKES THE NOSE OFF AND STANDS THERE, ANNOYED.

SCENE 2. INT. OPEN-PLAN OFFICE/RECEPTION AREA. DAY.

OFFICE SCENES: TRUDY IS WEARING DEELY-BOPPERS AND SHEILA IS SPORTING AN ILL-FITTING WONDERWOMAN OUTFIT. EVEN 'MONKEY' HAS JOINED IN THE ENFORCED MERRIMENT AND IS SPORTING A RED NOSE.

BRENT IS POINTING TO DAWN, WHO IS SITTING BEHIND RECEPTION WEARING RED LIPSTICK AND WITH HER HAIR IN BUNCHES. A D.I.Y. SIGN SAYS "KISSES FOR £1!"

BRENT: (to camera)
Everyone's joining in. This young lady. Ooh –
(POINTING AT SIGN)
– a bit saucy, selling kisses, for the lads – or the ladies, if there's any ladies that like that sort of … I don't think there are any in this office and if there are, good luck to them: they're all welcome, we're all equal now, so … It's different for girls anyway. It's more light-hearted, lower risk …

<u>GARETH:</u>
Erotic …

<u>BRENT:</u> (hearing GARETH, then pointing at DAWN)
Well, not in this case.
(REALISING WHAT HE'S SAID)
I mean it's not a sexual day. It's, er, you know …

CHRIS FINCH WALKS IN.

<u>BRENT:</u> (laughing, to camera)
Oh, you thought it was bad before – here's the man: Finchy!

FINCHY NOTICES DAWN'S SIGN.

<u>FINCH:</u>
Brentmeister!

<u>BRENT:</u>
Here we go.

<u>FINCH:</u>
Oh, kisses for a quid.

<u>BRENT:</u>
Oh. He's seen it!

<u>FINCH:</u>
It's a good cause. Do you mind kissing me on the nose?

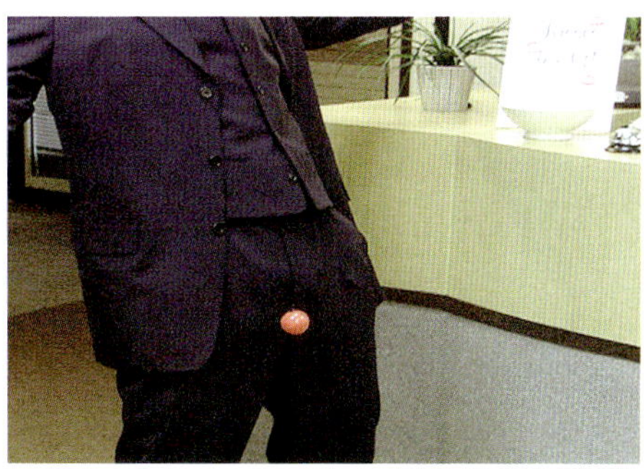

<u>DAWN:</u>
No. Put your quid in.

HE OPENS HIS JACKET. HE'S WEARING A RED NOSE IN HIS FLIES.

<u>FINCH:</u>
Okay. Kiss me on the nose!

BRENT AND GARETH CRACK UP.

<u>FINCH:</u> (to BRENT)
Hey, what do I get for a tenner?

<u>BRENT:</u>
Oh no.

HE SLAPS A TENNER ON THE RECEPTION DESK AND MIMES VIOLENT SHAGGING, COMPLETE WITH PELVIC THRUSTS THAT LEAVE LITTLE TO THE IMAGINATION.

<u>FINCH:</u>
Squeal, piggy, squeal!

FINCH'S SIMULATED RUTTING CONTINUES FOR QUITE SOME TIME. DAWN LOOKS ON IN DISBELIEF. BRENT AND GARETH FIND THIS ONE OF THE FUNNIEST THINGS THEY'VE EVER SEEN – THEY'LL BE TALKING ABOUT IT FOR WEEKS.

NOT BEFORE TIME, FINCH STOPS AND TAKES HIS TENNER BACK.

<u>FINCH:</u>
No, I'm not that desperate.

<u>BRENT:</u> (laughing, to camera)
Oh, who says famine has to be depressing?

BRENT DOES SOME LITTLE PELVIC THRUSTS OF HIS OWN.

<u>SCENE 3. INT. OPEN-PLAN OFFICE. DAY.</u>

TIM IS WORKING AT HIS DESK. GARETH HOPS OVER. TIM LOOKS ON, UNAMUSED. WE SEE THAT BEN, A SLOUGH EMPLOYEE, HAS HIS SUIT ON BACK TO FRONT.

SCENE 4. INT. OPEN-PLAN OFFICE. DAY.

TIM IS NOW TALKING TO THE CAMERA.

TIM:
Don't get me wrong, I've got nothing against this sort of thing. It's a good cause, but I just don't want to have to join in with someone else's idea of wackiness, okay? It's the wackiness I can't stand. It's like, you see someone outside Asda collecting for Cancer Research 'cos they've been personally affected by it, or whatever, or, I dunno, an old bloke selling poppies: there's a dignity about that. A real quiet dignity.

TIM LOOKS OVER HIS SHOULDER. GARETH AND BRENT AND A FEW OTHERS ARE WRESTLING BEN OFF HIS CHAIR.

TIM: (to camera)
And that's what today's all about. Dignity …

TIM LOOKS OVER HIS SHOULDER AGAIN. GARETH AND THE GANG HAVE NOW PULLED OFF BEN'S TROUSERS AND UNDERPANTS TO EXPOSE HIS PRIVATE PARTS TO THE CAMERA.

TIM: (to camera)
… always dignity.

BRENT AND GARETH ARE HAVING THE TIME OF THEIR LIFE.

BEN:
You bastards! My wife and kids are going to see those!

SCENE 5. INT. RECEPTION AREA. DAY.

BRENT IS STANDING WITH GARETH.

BRENT:
Sure. There's people watching this now, going: "Oi Brent, why are you still bothering with Comic Relief? They're always doing it and there's still people starving." That's why I'm still doing it; that's why you should too, you know …
(TO UNSEEN INTERVIEWER)
Probably put a number up there, shall we, if people wanna make donations?

BRENT HELPFULLY POINTS HIS FINGER TO INDICATE THE BOTTOM OF THE SCREEN.

BRENT:
And I hear people go, "Oh no, the money just goes to hungry foreigners." Not true. A lot of it stays in this country and goes to home-grown problems, a.k.a. –

BRENT HAS NOTICED BRENDA SITTING AT HER DESK IN HER WHEELCHAIR. HE GRABS HER CHAIR, PULLING HER BACKWARDS AND SWINGING HER ROUND TO FACE THE CAMERA.

BRENT:
– the disableds. You know, a lot of money goes to these fellas.
(TO BRENDA)
I'm not saying it goes to you, you know. You don't need it, do you? You're working. But – if you do claim for it, you probably claim for other stuff and that's up to you, as long as you don't abuse the system, you know.
(TO CAMERA)
Sadly a lot of them are.

BRENDA:
What do you mean?

BRENT:
A lot of people are abusing the system.

TIM IS AT HIS DESK, LISTENING.

GARETH: (chipping in)
You've got to make sure that the people who say that they're crippled –

BRENT: (correcting him)
– disabled –

GARETH:
– actually are –

BRENT:
– disabled.

BRENDA:
What? Are you suggesting that people pretend to be disabled in order to claim money off the DSS?

GARETH:
I don't know, I'm just saying there should be tests, that's all.

TIM:
Oh God. What tests?

GARETH:
Well, stick pins in their legs – see if they react …

BRENDA:
That is not going to work. I have feelings in my legs, I just can't walk.

GARETH:
Alright. I'm just saying there should be tests.

TIM:
We're all ears, Gareth.

GARETH:
Oh, I don't know. When they go down the DSS to make a claim, they should set off a fire alarm, a fake fire alarm. Everybody legs it out of the office, leaving them there. If they're a fake they'll be up and running with you; if they're real, they'll be left there … screaming … for help –

TIM REACTS.

<u>GARETH:</u>
– and then you just come back in and say, "It's alright, don't cry; it's just a test. You've passed – here's your money."

<u>BRENT:</u>
Yeah, spend it on what you like, one of those little blue cars or whatever you want …

SILENCE.

<u>GARETH:</u>
That's just one idea.

<u>BRENT:</u>
Yeah. So that's …

BRENT POINTS TO BRENDA, WHO IS WEARING SOME NOVELTY RED DEVIL HORNS.

<u>BRENT:</u>
She's joining in with it.
(PATRONISING)
Do you wanna put this on, a little nose?

<u>BRENDA:</u>
No I don't …

<u>BRENT:</u>
No. It's up to you.
(TO CAMERA)
Up to her. Her own decisions.

<u>SCENE 6. INT. OPEN-PLAN OFFICE. DAY.</u>

TIM AND GARETH ARE AT THEIR DESKS.

<u>TIM:</u>
Gareth, you know I'm doing kisses for a pound as well, like Dawn?

GARETH:
Well, you're not and I wouldn't pay if you were.

TIM:
I know, so I'll put your pound in, shall I?

GARETH:
Huh?

TIM:
I'll put a pound in so you can kiss me.

GARETH:
Look, I wouldn't kiss you if you paid me.

TIM:
Well, I am paying Gareth, it's quite simple. So first of all, just as it's for charity, I need to just get what's rightfully …

TIM CREEPS TOWARDS GARETH AND TRIES TO KISS HIM. GARETH FIGHTS HIM OFF.

GARETH:
Why are you such a bender? Get off of me.

TIM:
I'm not a bender, I'm just –

GARETH:
Get off.

TIM:
I'm not –

GARETH:
I'm not kissing you. I didn't put a pound in.

TIM:
Well, I'm gonna put a pound in.

GARETH:
You are such a pervert.

<u>TIM:</u>
I'm not a pervert.

<u>GARETH:</u>
A dirty little pervert.

<u>TIM:</u>
It just feels good though, that feels better …

<u>GARETH:</u>
Get off me.
(TO CAMERA)
I hope you're getting all this.

<u>TIM:</u>
I hope you're getting all this.

<u>GARETH:</u>
And I hope your girlfriend knows that you're gay 'cos otherwise she's gonna get a big surprise.

<u>TIM:</u> (poking around in GARETH's pocket)
Hang on, is that your big surprise? I've got your big surprise!

<u>GARETH:</u>
Get off!

<u>TIM:</u>
I've got it. I've found his big surprise. Oh, okay, alright, okay, okay, don't …

TIM BACKS OFF.

<u>GARETH:</u>
You take things too far.

<u>TIM:</u>
Alright. Just don't … Don't get so het up about it.

JUST WHEN GARETH THINKS HIS ORDEAL IS OVER, TIM GRABS HIM AND KISSES HIM FULL ON THE LIPS.

TIM:
Ha ha ha, hoo hoo hoo!

TIM MAKES FACES. DAWN IS HIGHLY AMUSED BY THESE ANTICS. GARETH WIPES HIS MOUTH CLEAN IN DISGUST.

GARETH: (to camera)
That was one-way. I didn't kiss him back.

SCENE 7. INT. OPEN-PLAN OFFICE. DAY.

VARIOUS EMPLOYEES ARE STANDING IN A LINE TRYING TO PASS AN ORANGE TO ONE ANOTHER UNDER THEIR CHINS.

BRENT IS LAST IN THE LINE AND TRUDY IS NEXT TO HIM. NATURALLY, BRENT IS EXCITED AT THE THOUGHT OF THE INTIMACY, BUT JUST AS SHE IS ABOUT TO PASS THE ORANGE TO BRENT, JENNIFER TAYLOR-CLARKE WALKS INTO THE OFFICE.

JENNIFER:
Okay, gather round everybody. We've got a little surprise for you. Do you want to come away from your desks?

TRUDY HASTILY DROPS THE ORANGE, AND SHE AND THE REST OF THE LINE WALK OFF TOWARDS JENNIFER.

BRENT IS LEFT, CROUCHING, WAITING FOR THE ORANGE.

BRENT: (disgruntled, calling after them)
On my turn! Can you remember where we were in that game?

ANGRY AND FRUSTRATED, HE KICKS THE ORANGE AWAY LIKE A MOODY CHILD.

<u>JENNIFER:</u> (to SHEILA)
Sheila. Oh Sheila, nice costume. You look fantastic.
(TO EVERYONE)
Okay, would you please give a big warm welcome to the fantastic Neil Godwin and the lovely Rachel!

NEIL ENTERS, DRESSED IN A WHITE SUIT LIKE JOHN TRAVOLTA IN *SATURDAY NIGHT FEVER*. RACHEL IS WITH HIM, WEARING A RED 1970S DRESS.

<u>NEIL:</u>
It's that time again. Now, we've both suffered for our art here. Please would you mind suffering with us and I'm going to be collecting at the end, so if you could give generously? Thanks very much. Jennifer, could you do the honours please?

BRENT IS LISTENING TO THIS. HE LOOKS WORRIED. NEIL IS STEALING HIS LIMELIGHT.

JENNIFER HITS 'PLAY' ON THE STEREO. IT'S 'MORE THAN A WOMAN' BY THE BEE-GEES.

PEOPLE GATHER ROUND AND START WHOOPING AND CHEERING AS NEIL AND RACHEL BEGIN A CHOREOGRAPHED DANCE APEING THE ONE IN *SATURDAY NIGHT FEVER*. IT'S ROUGH AND READY BUT GOOD ENOUGH TO IMPRESS THE STAFF OF A PAPER MERCHANTS IN SLOUGH.

WE CUTAWAY TO: BRENT LOOKING IRRITATED. OTHER PEOPLE ARE SMILING AND CLAPPING. TIM IS LOOKING AT RACHEL ADMIRINGLY. DAWN IS WATCHING TIM WATCHING RACHEL. BRENT IS WATCHING NEIL WITH INCREASING JEALOUSY AND ANNOYANCE.

THE MUSIC SEGUES INTO 'YOU SHOULD BE DANCING' AND NEIL PICKS UP THE TEMPO, DOING A SOLO DISCO-DANCE ROUTINE COMPLETE WITH POINTS, TWIRLS AND HAND-JIVES.

BRENT:
That looks gay.

THE CROWD ARE LOVING IT.

THE MUSIC FINISHES AND THE ROOM GOES WILD, CHEERING, CLAPPING, WHISTLING.

RACHEL RUNS OVER TO TIM, EXCITED AND PROUD. HE HUGS HER IN FRONT OF DAWN, WHO DOESN'T QUITE KNOW WHERE TO LOOK OR WHAT TO DO WITH HERSELF.

NEIL HAS A CHARITY BUCKET AND STARTS COLLECTING MONEY AND PRAISE. BRENT LOOKS SICK WITH JEALOUSY.

NEIL:
Thank you very much. There's quite a bit in there. You can add that to yours if you like.

BRENT:
Cheers. I've already raised more than that in a way.
(TO CAMERA)
Three hundred quid we did last time, so er …
(TO NEIL)
And if you wanted dancing you should've come to me, couldn't you, if you want? I know you rehearsed that, it's all planned.

NEIL:
What, do you dance?

BRENT:
Big time. More modern stuff than that as well. I sort of fused Flashdance with MC Hammer shit.

RACHEL:
Alright then mate, well, show us your moves.

BRENT:
No, there's no beat, is there?

NEIL:
Oh, go on.

BRENT:
You had music and everything. Well … as it's for charity, just a little bit.

BRENT STARTS JIGGING AROUND AND CLAPPING. EVERYONE STARTS CLAPPING AND HUMMING AS HE BEGINS HIS DANCE.

IT IS THE MOST LUDICROUS THING ANYONE HAS EVER SEEN. SOMEHOW THEIR BOSS IS TRYING TO INCORPORATE BREAK, DISCO AND BOY-BAND DANCE MOVES INTO ONE FLUID WHOLE. LIKE A TRAFFIC ACCIDENT, NO-ONE REALLY WANTS TO LOOK BUT THEY ARE INCAPABLE OF AVERTING THEIR EYES. THE CLAPPING FIZZLES OUT AND EVERYONE IN THE ROOM GAZES IN WIDE-EYED WONDER AT BRENT'S 'ROUTINE'. HE ATTEMPTS A FINAL TWIRL AND ENDS WITH A FLOURISH.

BRENT:
So, and that's …

EVERYONE FEELS OBLIGED TO APPLAUD, WEAKLY.

TIM:
Great, David.

BRENT:
Give me a bit of warning next time and you might get a …

GARETH:
We don't have to give a donation for that, do we?

BRENT:
Well, don't say it like that. All the money collected is for both dances, both excellent dances in their … If there is a difference, mine was impromptu, so … But I don't think you should get extra points for that necessarily. Make your own minds up, leave me out of it. I'm collecting for charity. Alright?

HE PICKS UP THE CHARITY BUCKET AND STROLLS OFF, LEAVING HIS AUDIENCE SPEECHLESS.

BRENT TALKING HEAD. INT. DAY.

BRENT:

You've seen me entertain and raise money, but maybe I'd like to do that in the future for a living. You know, use my humour and my profile to both help and amuse people and if it's ideas for TV shows, game shows or whatever you want, I'm your man. I'm already exploring the entertainment avenue with my management training, but I'd like to do that on a global scale really. And that's not going, "Oh look at me today, I'm entertaining whilst saving lives – aren't I brilliant?" It's going, "If you think I'm brilliant, then give generously and help save these guys who are starving but are also brilliant". Not as entertainers – a lot of them can't even speak English – but, you know, don't give them their own game show, but save them from dying at least. And then maybe they could do something in their own country, on television or whatever they have – the wireless – or, I don't know, some ... Give 'em a job on the world service or summat.

SCENE 8. INT. RECEPTION AREA. DAY.

'JIMMY THE PERV' AND 'THE OGGMONSTER' ARRIVE. THEY'RE CRAZY-LOOKING GUYS WEARING LONG WHITE COATS AND WITH STETHOSCOPES ROUND THEIR NECKS. 'JIMMY THE PERV' HAS A CHARITY BUCKET. 'THE OGGMONSTER' RINGS DAWN'S DESK BELL EXCITEDLY.

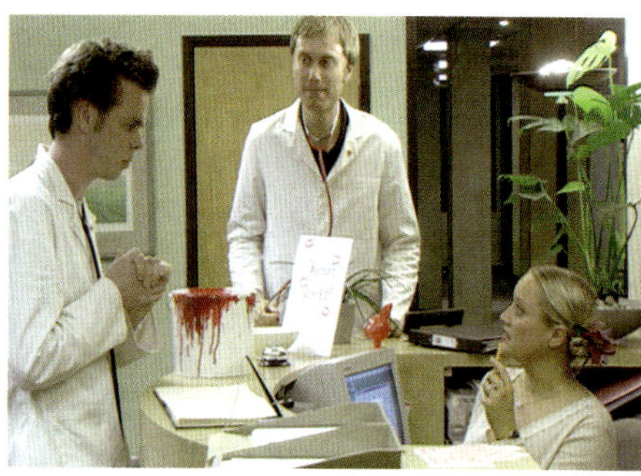

JIMMY THE PERV:

Right, we're from the local mental hospital. Is Gareth Keenan here, 'cos he's escaped!

<u>OGGY:</u>
'Cos he is mental.

WE CUT TO GARETH, EXCITED AND LAUGHING.

<u>GARETH:</u>
It's my crew.

TIM REACTS. GARETH HOPS OVER TO JOIN HIS 'CREW'.

<u>JIMMY THE PERV:</u> (to DAWN)
Kisses for a quid. Yes, I'll have some, thank you very much.

<u>GARETH:</u>
My mad mates, that's all we need!

JIMMY THE PERV GIVES DAWN A QUID FOR A KISS. SHE KISSES HIM. HE GIVES HER ANOTHER POUND FROM HIS CHARITY BUCKET. SHE KISSES HIM. HE GIVES HER ANOTHER QUID.

<u>DAWN:</u>
Oh, lovely. Um …

<u>JIMMY THE PERV:</u>
Another one.

HE CONTINUES TO GIVE HER POUND COINS, WITH EACH ATTEMPTED KISS BECOMING MORE LASCIVIOUS.

<u>GARETH:</u> (to DAWN)
My mates.

TIM REACTS.

<u>GARETH:</u>
Sorry about this. My mad mates.

BRENT APPEARS. HE NOTICES THE WHITE COATS.

<u>BRENT:</u> (to GARETH)
They've finally come to take you away then?

<u>JIMMY THE PERV:</u>
Are you mad as well?

<u>BRENT:</u>
Guilty.

<u>GARETH:</u>
He's the boss.

<u>JIMMY THE PERV:</u>
Oh, give us a job.

<u>BRENT:</u> (gesturing to GARETH)
I've already got one reprobate, thanks very much.

<u>GARETH:</u> (introducing his 'crew')
Jimmy the Perv and the Oggmonster.

BRENT IMMEDIATELY CLOCKS THAT THE OGGMONSTER IS VERY TALL.

<u>BRENT:</u> (looking up at OGGY)
Oh, bloody hell. What's the weather like up there?

<u>OGGY:</u>
Oh, I've heard that before.

<u>BRENT:</u>
Parents put you in a grow bag when you were little, did they?

<u>OGGY:</u>
That's an old one.

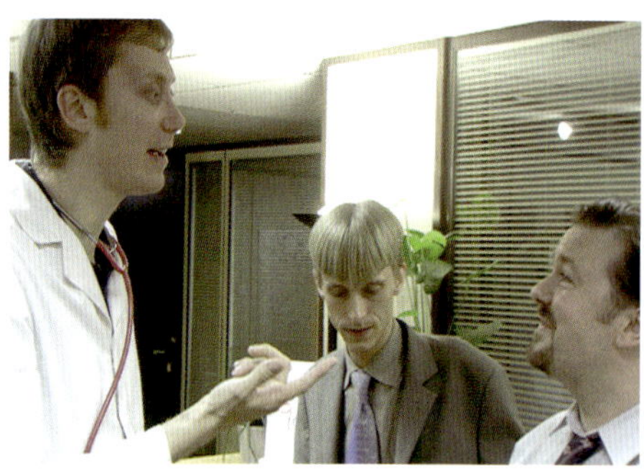

<u>BRENT:</u>
"Let's grow ourselves a big lanky goggle-eyed freak of a son."

<u>OGGY:</u>
Alright, calm down mate. There's no need to get offensive.

BRENT:
No, no, I was joining –

OGGY:
I didn't call you fatty as soon as I saw you.

BRENT:
Alright. No, I was joining in with –

OGGY:
No. And don't have a go at the eyes, because that is a stigmatism that I've had from the age of five so that's what makes them a bit bulbous, so don't just … I didn't call you like whale man or the blubber man as soon as I saw you!

BRENT:
No, yeah, but I don't go round calling myself 'the mong boy'.

OGGY:
Well, I don't either. I call myself 'the Oggmonster'.

BRENT:
I'm not going to call you 'the Oggmonster'.

OGGY:
Well, that's my name.

BRENT:
No it's not. What's your real name?

OGGY:
Nathan.

BRENT:
That's a good name.

OGGY: (tearful)
Is it?

BRENT:
Yes. I'll call you Nathan.

<u>OGGY:</u>
I didn't call you fatty soon as I saw you.

HE RUNS OFF IN TEARS.

<u>BRENT:</u>
What is … What is the matter with him?

EVERYONE STANDS IN SILENCE, LOOKING AWKWARD. TIM REACTS.

<u>SCENE 9. INT. OPEN-PLAN OFFICE. DAY.</u>

TIM IS WALKING OVER TO TWO OF HIS COLLEAGUES.

<u>TIM:</u> (to camera)
I've got a sponsorship form for Comic Relief. I wanted to enter into the spirit a bit more, you know, so … Erm, gents, sorry to interrupt –
(TO EMPLOYEES)
– I wonder if you'd like to sponsor me? I have to hide as many of Gareth's possessions as I can from him for the rest of the day.

<u>OLIVER:</u>
You've got to do what?

<u>TIM:</u>
I will be hiding Gareth's belongings.

<u>EMPLOYEE:</u>
I'll give you two quid for the lot.

<u>TIM:</u>
Two quid for the lot. Yes, a most generous offer.

SCENE 10. INT. BRENT'S OFFICE. DAY.

BRENT WALKS INTO HIS OFFICE AND FINDS JENNIFER AND NEIL ARE ALREADY IN THERE.

BRENT:
They're waiting for me. Ooh, break it up, put her down. No, they wouldn't – she wouldn't … Her husband's loaded, isn't he?

JENNIFER:
He does okay.

BRENT:
Ohhh, dear … Oh, what a day.

BRENT POINTS AND LAUGHS AT THE JOHN TRAVOLTA SUIT THAT NEIL IS STILL WEARING.

NEIL: (friendly)
Okay David, do you have that report?

BRENT LOOKS A LITTLE LOST.

BRENT: (stalling)
Oh, glad you've brought that up …

NEIL:
Well, that's why I'm here.

BRENT:
Yes, um, I'm formulating a lot of good ideas that are …

NEIL:
No, David, I don't want to talk about a report, or the report we're gonna do soon, I'm talking about the report that we talked about four days ago that was definitely going to be done today. You know how important I consider this report to be. I come in and I discover that this –

NEIL PICKS UP A PIECE OF PAPER FROM BRENT'S DESK AND WAVES IT UNDER HIS NOSE.

<u>NEIL:</u>
– is the fruit of your labours.

<u>BRENT:</u>
Well, don't go through my stuff when I'm not here.

<u>NEIL:</u>
Just please read the first sentence.

<u>BRENT:</u>
Well ...

<u>NEIL:</u>
Just please read the first sentence for Jennifer.

<u>BRENT:</u> (reading)
"Imagine a cross between Telly Addicts and Noel's House Party. You've just imagined Upstairs Downstairs, a new quiz show devised and hosted by David Brent."

<u>NEIL:</u>
David, I just don't understand this.

<u>BRENT:</u>
Well, the contestants run upstairs and they get a clue and then –

<u>NEIL:</u>
No. Not the game show. I don't understand why you haven't done the report you said you'd do. I don't understand your consistent negligence, and failure to do what is asked of you.

<u>BRENT:</u>
Because you're viewing my methods like there's something missing, like you're looking at it like the jigsaw that it is, but you're viewing it through a keyhole when really you should be –

BRENT MAKES AN EXPANDING MOTION WITH HIS HANDS.

<u>NEIL:</u>
David, some words would be useful here.

<u>BRENT:</u>
Oh, I think actions speak louder than words.

NEIL:
You're on a warning. That's the action I'm going to take, it's a verbal warning – obviously, three strikes and you're out – and things have got to change.

BRENT:
Fine. Give me all three now then, because, oh, I'd love to see you run this place. You'd have a mutiny on your hands for a start 'cos they would … If that's what you want, come on! Let's bring it on and I'll be out …

NEIL:
No, David, that's not what I want. I wanna see this place run with you doing your job, okay? Take the verbal warning –

BRENT:
– Still take the warning? –

NEIL:
– take the verbal warning, learn from it and let's move onwards and upwards. Okay?

BRENT SHRUGS.

BRENT TALKING HEAD. INT. DAY.

BRENT:
Neil makes me laugh though because, you know, it's his interfering, it's his timing. He's going on about he wants some report doing – it's Red Nose day, you know? Ooh, what's more important? You, "Neil" …
(HE MIMES THE INVERTED COMMAS)
… with your "report" …
(MORE INVERTED COMMAS)
… or some starving children?
(SCRATCHING HIS CHIN)
Ooh, I don't know. What would Lenny Henry say? I think we know. Imagine him going out of the door on Comic Relief day and Dawn French is going:

(NAGGING VOICE)
"Where you going? You haven't done the washing-up, you haven't put the rubbish out."
(GIVING THE FINGER, OVERLY ANGRY)
"Do it yourself, I've gotta save some Africans."

SCENE 11. INT. SMOKERS' ROOM. DAY.

KEITH IS SITTING IN THE SMOKERS' ROOM, STILL DRESSED AS ALI G. DAWN IS THUMBING THROUGH A MAGAZINE.

KEITH:
What are you reading?

DAWN:
A holiday brochure.

KEITH:
Why's that then? Going on holiday?

DAWN:
Possibly.

KEITH:
Where to?

DAWN:
The States.

PAUSE.

KEITH:
United States?

DAWN:
Yep.

LONG PAUSE.

KEITH:
I don't know if you've heard the gossip but Tim's going out with Rachel.

DAWN:
Yeah, yeah I'd heard.

KEITH:
Yeah. 'Cos he used to fancy you, didn't he?

DAWN:
Oh, did he?

KEITH:
Yeah, yeah, yeah. He did. And now he's found someone better.

DAWN:
Yep.

ANOTHER LONG PAUSE.

SCENE 12. INT. OPEN-PLAN OFFICE. DAY.

GARETH HOPS OVER AND SITS AT HIS DESK. HE GOES TO MAKE A PHONE CALL BUT CANNOT FIND HIS PHONE.

GARETH:
Have you seen my phone? Where is my phone?

TIM TRIES NOT TO LAUGH. GARETH REALISES THAT SOMETHING IS AFOOT.

GARETH:
Have you got it? Where have you put it? Seriously, where have you put my phone? I don't believe it.

TIM:
Gareth?

GARETH:
So many times I've told you not to touch my stuff.

GARETH GETS UP AND BEGINS SEARCHING TIM'S DESK FOR TRACES OF HIS PHONE.

TIM:
Gareth, listen. Excuse me.

GARETH:
The phone's a different matter.

TIM:
Gareth, it's for charity...

GARETH: (still searching)
What else have you taken?

TIM:
I haven't taken –

GARETH:
Where's my Tiny Tanks?

TIM HOOTS WITH LAUGHTER.

GARETH:
How am I supposed to work?

TIM:
You'll just have to hop to it …

SCENE 13. INT. SMOKERS' ROOM. DAY.

KEITH AND DAWN ARE STILL SITTING THERE IN SILENCE.

KEITH:
A lot of crime in America.

DAWN:
Right, well, I'll be careful.

KEITH:
Word of advice: keep your traveller's cheques in a bum-bag.

DAWN:
Thanks. I'll … I'll buy one.

KEITH:
What, when you get there?

DAWN:
Yep.

<u>KEITH:</u> (sighing)
Word of warning then: out there they call them 'fanny packs' ...

PAUSE.

<u>KEITH:</u>
... 'cos fanny means your arse over there ...

PAUSE.

<u>KEITH:</u>
... not your minge.

DAWN REACTS. KEITH TAKES A BITE FROM A SCOTCH EGG.

<u>SCENE 14. INT. OPEN-PLAN OFFICE. DAY.</u>

TIM IS SITTING AT HIS DESK WORKING. GARETH HOPS IN AGAIN.

HIS ENTIRE DESK HAS BEEN CLEARED OF ALL HIS BELONGINGS. ALL THAT REMAINS IS A RED NOSE AND THE MOUSE OF HIS COMPUTER. THE REST OF THE COMPUTER IS MISSING, ALONG WITH EVERYTHING ELSE.

<u>GARETH:</u>
Where is ... ? God ... You're so immature ... Where ... ? Right: I demand that everything –

IN HIS FURY, GARETH STOPS HOPPING.

<u>TIM:</u> (shouting to the room)
Gareth has stopped hopping, everyone!

FRUSTRATED BY HIS OWN RULES, GARETH BEGINS HOPPING AGAIN.

<u>GARETH:</u> (surveying his empty desk)
How am I supposed to do any work?

<u>TIM:</u>
Gareth, I've told you, it's for charity.

<u>GARETH:</u>
It's not for charity though, is it? It's for you winding me up. And you've been doing it again.

EXHAUSTED, GARETH STOPS HOPPING.

<u>TIM:</u> (shouting to the room)
Gareth's stopped hopping again!

<u>GARETH:</u>
I don't have to hop all day. It's just when I'm moving that I have to hop.

<u>TIM:</u>
Where does it say that in the rule book?

<u>GARETH:</u>
Where is my … ? See, that's mine, for a start, straight away. Where's the rest of it?

DAWN LOOKS ON, SMILING.

<u>TIM:</u>
Gareth, Gareth, okay Gareth, just calm down, okay? Have a seat: you've been on your foot all day.

<u>GARETH:</u> (off-screen)
Oh God, how do you hide a chair?

<u>SCENE 15. INT. RECEPTION AREA. DAY.</u>

TIM WALKS UP TO DAWN AND DROPS SOMETHING IN THE POST TRAY. THEY CHAT, BUT IT'S NOT THE USUAL FLIRTING. IT'S FRIENDLY BUT WORK-RELATED.

<u>TIM:</u>
Dawney, take that?

DAWN:
Yeah, sure.

TIM:
You alright?

DAWN:
Yeah, you?

LEE COMES IN WITH DAWN'S LUNCH IN A BAG.

TIM:
Hello.

LEE:
There you go. Prawn and avocado.

DAWN:
Thank you.

LEE:
See you later on.

DAWN:
Yeah. Are you not going to eat here?

LEE:
No, I've got to get back.

DAWN:
Oh, well. I've made nineteen pounds today.

LEE:
Yeah? Any of it going to English kids or is it all going abroad, I suppose?

TIM:
Well, just … Will you please stop moaning and give her a quid for a kiss.

LEE:
I'm not paying for it, mate.

TIM:
Listen, listen, them's the rules, look.

DAWN:
Thank you.

LEE PUTS IN A FIVER.

LEE:
There you go. What do I get for that? Come here, you.

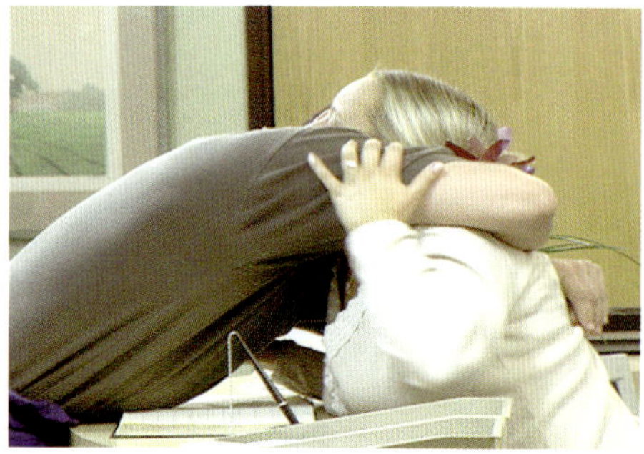

HE GOES TO KISS HER BUT INSTEAD PRETENDS TO BITE HER NECK. SHE LAUGHS AND THEY PLAY-FIGHT.

TIM WATCHES. IT'S HIS TURN TO FEEL AWKWARD AND NOT KNOW WHERE TO LOOK.

TIM:
Oh good. That's great.

LEE SAYS HIS GOODBYES, PRETENDS TO TAKE DAWN'S COLLECTION, THEN PUTS IT BACK. HE LEAVES HER, SMILING.

TIM IS LEFT WITH DAWN.

TIM:
Right, oh, my contribution.

HE DROPS A POUND IN HER COLLECTION PLATE.

DAWN:
Thank you. Where do you want your kiss?

TIM:
Uh?

DAWN:
Where do you want your kiss?

TIM:
No, it's alright, I'll just … give you a pound.

DAWN:
You've got to have a kiss.

TIM:
I don't have to have a kiss –

DAWN GRABS TIM'S LAPELS, PULLS HIM TOWARDS HER AND KISSES HIM SQUARE ON THE LIPS. IT'S A LITTLE TOO TENDER AND LINGERING TO BE ENTIRELY PLATONIC. THEY PULL APART, AVOIDING EACH OTHER'S EYES.

TIM WANDERS BACK TO HIS SEAT.

THE CAMERA STAYS ON DAWN.

SCENE 16. INT. OPEN-PLAN OFFICE. DAY.

OFFICE SCENES. TIM IS BACK AT HIS DESK BUT LOOKS PENSIVE. GARETH HAS NOW FOUND HIS COMPUTER.

RACHEL WANDERS OVER TO TIM'S DESK.

RACHEL:
What are you doing?

TIM:
Just working.

RACHEL:
I'm very, very, very bored.

SHE PUSHES HIS STUFF ASIDE AND SITS ON HIS DESK, SMILING AT HIM.

GARETH:
Excuse me. Desk procedures. Chairs are for sitting on.

RACHEL: (to TIM)
I think he's a little bit jealous that he's not getting the view you're getting.

GARETH:
Wrong: I've got the arse this side so I'd only wanna be sitting where he's sitting if you was wearing a skirt – then I could look up there … at it.

RACHEL: (to TIM)
Aren't you going to defend my honour?

TIM: (laughing, embarrassed)
No … I think you … you'd better get off the table.

RACHEL:
Ooh, he's getting a bit embarrassed by his new girlfriend.

TIM TRIES TO LAUGH THIS OFF BUT HE CLEARLY IS EMBARRASSED.

TIM:
I'm not.

RACHEL:
You are.

TIM:
I'm not. I'm not.

RACHEL:
You alright?

TIM:
Yeah.

SHE KISSES HIM ON THE CHEEK AND GETS OFF THE DESK.

RACHEL:
You cool?

TIM GIVES A THUMBS-UP BUT LOOKS TROUBLED.

SCENE 17. INT. BRENT'S OFFICE. DAY.

NEIL AND JENNIFER KNOCK AND ENTER. BRENT IS SITTING BEHIND HIS DESK.

NEIL:
Excuse me, David, erm …

BRENT:
Yes.

NEIL:
Can we have another quick word?

BRENT:
Not now, no. I'm literally running downstairs this minute.

NEIL:
What for?

BRENT:
The Gazette are coming in to take my picture, so I'm going to be in the paper – well, Wernham Hogg are gonna be in the paper. Free advertising, so … That's not why I'm doing it.

NEIL:
This shouldn't take long.

BRENT:
Okay.

NEIL:
I'm sorry to spring this on you now: we've been discussing something that you said earlier and it's certainly something we've been thinking about as well. We would like to offer you a very generous redundancy package.

BRENT IS DUMBFOUNDED.

BRENT:
Are you offering me it or are you telling me I've got to take it?

NEIL:
Um … We're telling you you've got to take it.

JENNIFER:
We will put in a proper meeting tomorrow.

BRENT:
That's good timing, innit? Telling me that today – the day of laughter. Brilliant. Well, that's that ruined, isn't it?

BRENT STANDS UP. HE'S WEARING A BERNIE CLIFTON OSTRICH COSTUME.

BRENT:
That's what I was … It's got pockets and everything.

HE STANDS IN SILENCE, GUTTED, DIGESTING THE NEWS.

BRENT:
So now I've got to try and go down there and be funny. It's gonna be good, innit, with that going through –
(HE POINTS TO HIS HEAD WITH THE BEAK OF THE OSTRICH)
I knew you were up to something, planning something.
(TO JENNIFER)
Jennifer do you agree with this because we can …

JENNIFER NODS.

BRENT:
I'll be alright. Don't worry about me. I've got other irons in the fire, so this is the best thing that's ever happened to me, to be honest.

BRENT IS HOLDING THE OSTRICH HEAD WITH A STICK. WHEN HE MOTIONS AS HE TALKS, THE OSTRICH HEAD FLIPS AROUND LIKE IT'S ALIVE.

BRENT:
But I'm going to love to see you telling that lot out there because you are going to have a mutiny on your hands. They will go berserk. Definitely.

THEY SAY NOTHING.

BRENT:
If that's it, can you leave now please? Go on. I've got stuff to do. I've got, I've got laughter … I've got money to raise … mouths to feed.

NEIL:
Thanks for your time.

BRENT:
Yeah.

NEIL AND JENNIFER LEAVE.

BRENT'S NOT SURE WHAT TO DO. HE GOES OUT INTO THE OFFICE AND ADDRESSES THE ROOM.

BRENT:
Um … If you're wondering what that meeting was just about in there … That's it … I've been made redundant. Yeah. After it was me who saved others from redundancy and then it's back … The good die young! I said you lot'd go mental.

EVERYONE LOOKS BLANK.

BRENT:
And now I've got to go and give laughter … But … See ya …

HE STARTS TO WALK OFF THEN TURNS ROUND, EXPECTING A REACTION.

BRENT:
Huh?

BUT PEOPLE JUST STARE AT HIM BLANKLY.

HE WALKS OUT OF THE OFFICE, STILL IN COSTUME.

SCENE 18. EXT. CAR PARK. DAY.

A PHOTOGRAPHER IS PREPARING TO TAKE PHOTOS OF BRENT IN HIS OSTRICH OUTFIT.

DAWN AND TIM ARE WRAPPED IN COATS, LOOKING COLD AND MISERABLE, AND HOLDING A BIG CHEQUE THAT SAYS "£120".

IT'S MURKY AND OVERCAST.

PHOTOGRAPHER:
Okay. Do you just want to make it peck?

BRENT MAKES THE OSTRICH PECK AT THE FLOOR.

PHOTOGRAPHER:
Yeah. Just run around a bit? Yeah.

BRENT RUNS AROUND. HE LOOKS PITIFUL.

PHOTOGRAPHER:
Good. Yeah. Good. Okay. Smile: it's for Comic Relief.

BRENT:
Can I just do it standing here?

PHOTOGRAPHER:
Yeah. Just, can you make it peck at your mates, like Roy Hudd.

BRENT:
Rod Hull.

PHOTOGRAPHER:
Yeah, just do that.

BRENT MAKES THE OSTRICH HEAD PECK TIM.

PHOTOGRAPHER:
Good. Yeah. Okay. Good, that's fine, yeah, it's a bit dark actually, I didn't bring a flash. Probably won't be able to use these actually. Okay. Don't be disappointed if they're not in.

BRENT: (deflated)
No.

PHOTOGRAPHER:
Okay.

TIM:
Thank you.

PHOTOGRAPHER:
Cheers.

DAWN:
Bye. Well done David.

THE PHOTOGRAPHER LEAVES.

TIM:
Well done, mate.

BRENT:
No worries.

GARETH HOPS INTO VIEW.

GARETH:
Did I miss it?

CLOSING MUSIC AND END CREDITS, THEN:

THE PHONE RINGS IN THE ACCOUNTS DEPARTMENT. KEITH, STILL IN COSTUME, ANSWERS IT.

KEITH: (unexpressive)
Booyakasha.

Episode **Six**

CAST
David Brent RICKY GERVAIS
Tim MARTIN FREEMAN
Gareth MACKENZIE CROOK
Dawn LUCY DAVIS
Neil PATRICK BALADI
Rachel STACEY ROCA

with
Lee JOEL BECKETT
Helena OLIVIA COLMAN
Jennifer STIRLING GALLACHER
Ray TOM GOODMAN-HILL
Jude JENNIFER HENNESEY
Keith EWEN MACKINTOSH
Jamie JAMIE DEEKS

and
Ben Bradshaw, Patrick Driver,
Julie Fernandez, Rachel Isaac,
Jane Lucas, Tony MacMurray,
Emma Manton, Ron Merchant,
Alexander Perkins, Philip Pickard
and Howard Saddler

SCENE 1. INT. OPEN-PLAN OFFICE. DAY.

BRENT IS WANDERING AROUND THE OFFICE, HANDING OUT BUSINESS CARDS CONSPICUOUSLY.

HIS TALKING HEAD BEGINS OVER THIS.

BRENT TALKING HEAD. INT. DAY.

BRENT:
I don't look upon this like it's the end; I look upon it like it's moving on, you know? It's almost like my work here's done. I can't imagine Jesus going, "Oh, I've told a few people here in Bethlehem I'm the son of God; can I just stay here with mum and dad now?" "No, you've got to move on, you've got to spread the word. You've got to go to Nazareth please." And that's very much like ... me. My world does not end with these four walls. Slough's a big place, and when I'm finished with Slough there's Reading, Aldershot, Bracknell, you know, I've got Didcot, Yately. Winnersh. Taplow, you know? Because I am my own boss, I can – Burfield – I can wake up one morning and go, "Oh, I don't feel like working today, can I just stay in bed?" "Oh, I dunno, you'd better ask the boss." "David, can I stay in bed all day?" "Yes, you can, David."

HE POINTS TO HIMSELF.

BRENT:
Both me. I'm not ... That's not me in bed with another bloke called David.

SCENE 2. INT. OPEN-PLAN OFFICE. DAY.

BRENT CROUCHES DOWN NEXT TO JAMIE.

BRENT:
Be a bit weird for you, will it, when I'm …

JAMIE:
Well, different certainly …

BRENT:
Sadder, sadder, but I'm telling this to everyone: I do not want you going, "Oh that's it, we're out of here, there's no point", or walking round with your shoulders hunched –

JAMIE'S PHONE RINGS.

JAMIE:
Sorry, can I just get that?

BRENT:
Yeah.

JAMIE: (answering phone)
Hello? Oh that's great. No … That's a load off my mind … Thanks for calling. Cheers. Bye.

HE HANGS UP.

JAMIE: (to BRENT)
Sorry, what were you saying?

BRENT:
I was just, just … I want to, you know –

JAMIE: (interrupting)
Oliver?

OLIVER:
Hello.

JAMIE:
They took the lot, mate.

OLIVER:
All of it? You lucky … You were bricking it, weren't you?

<u>JAMIE:</u>
I was. Yeah.

<u>BRENT:</u>
All I'm saying is, um, I don't want you … I'll leave you with –

<u>JAMIE:</u> (to BRENT)
Sorry, can I just phone Steve?

<u>BRENT:</u>
Yeah. Busy. Too busy.

JAMIE MAKES ANOTHER CALL. BRENT TRIES TO GET UP SUBTLY.

<u>JAMIE:</u>
Steve, it's Jamie, they took the lot mate … Yeah … No, it's a team effort … Yeah … Oh well, that's what I thought …

BRENT PUTS HIS BUSINESS CARD DOWN IN FRONT OF JAMIE, BUT HE'S NOT INTERESTED.

HE SPOTS BIG KEITH AT THE PHOTOCOPIER.

<u>BRENT:</u> (cheery, to camera)
Oh, here he is. The big man.

BRENT STANDS BEHIND HIM, GETTING A BUSINESS CARD OUT OF HIS POCKET. BIG KEITH STEPS BACKWARDS AND, WITHOUT NOTICING, TREADS ON BRENT'S TOE. BRENT WINCES IN PAIN BUT TRIES TO RETAIN HIS DIGNITY.

<u>BRENT:</u>
Ahhh. Clumsy.

HE WALKS OFF.

SCENE 3. INT. OPEN-PLAN OFFICE. DAY.

OFFICE SHOTS. DAWN AND TIM ARE BOTH LOST IN THOUGHT.

RACHEL COMES OVER TO TIM'S DESK.

RACHEL:
Hiya.

TIM:
Hiya. Alright?

RACHEL:
How are you?

TIM:
I'm alright. How are you?

RACHEL:
My mum and dad phoned me last night –

TIM:
Uhuh.

RACHEL:
Um, okay, basically we have this beautiful little cottage in the New Forest. Once a year we kind of organise this family do and, um, my mum and dad wanted to know whether we'd like to come.

TIM:
Oh, what a shame, I can't. When is it?

RACHEL:
Well, we'll have about like a week, two weeks' notice or –

TIM:
Yeah, yeah, yeah, yeah, that's …

RACHEL:
It'll be on the weekend.

TIM:
That's what, yeah, that's tricky. That's a problem … potentially.

RACHEL:
Well, I kind of told them that we'd go.

TIM:
You told them? Well, I wish you'd asked me.

SCENE 4. INT. OPEN-PLAN OFFICE. DAY.

GARETH'S PHONE RINGS. HE PUTS IT ON SPEAKER-PHONE.

GARETH:
Hello?

OGGY: (on speaker-phone)
Oggy oggy oggy!

GARETH:
Oy oy oy!
(LAUGHING)
Alright Oggy? Keeno here, on speaker-phone.

OGGY:
You on speaker-phone?

GARETH:
Yeah.

OGGY:
Tits!

GARETH:
Shut up!

THEY BOTH LAUGH. TIM WATCHES THIS.

OGGY:
Who heard that?

<u>GARETH:</u>
Everyone, you mentalist. Shut up. What do you want?

<u>OGGY:</u>
You coming down Chasers tonight for Gobbler's birthday?

<u>GARETH:</u>
Yeah, definitely. Jimmy the Perv coming?

<u>OGGY:</u>
Yeah, yeah.

<u>GARETH:</u>
What about Fishfingers?

GARETH LOOKS AROUND, GRINNING, TO CHECK THAT PEOPLE HAVE HEARD THE NAME OF HIS CRAZY PAL.

<u>OGGY:</u>
Oh, Fishfingers can't come because Susan caught him getting off with what's-her-face with the norks –

<u>GARETH:</u>
Oh no. That is mental.

<u>OGGY:</u>
Yeah.

<u>GARETH:</u>
I'll see you later then.

<u>OGGY:</u>
Gonads!

OGGY HANGS UP. GARETH LAUGHS, LOOKING ROUND.

<u>GARETH:</u>
Mentalist. Did you hear that?

<u>TIM:</u>
Uhuh.

TIM HOLDS HIS HEAD IN HIS HANDS. HE IS STILL SPENDING HIS LIFE SITTING NEXT TO THIS MAN.

<u>GARETH:</u>
Oggmonster.

SCENE 5. INT. RECEPTION/OPEN-PLAN OFFICE. DAY.

BRENT WALKS INTO THE OFFICE WITH HELENA PIDGEON, A HORSEY-LOOKING YOUNG WOMAN, DRESSED IN A SUIT.

<u>BRENT:</u>
Here we are. The madhouse.
(TO DAWN)
Hiya.

BRENT LINGERS NEAR TIM.

<u>BRENT:</u>
Oh, alright Tim?

<u>TIM:</u>
Alright.

BRENT'S TRYING TO GET HELENA NOTICED.

<u>BRENT:</u>
What her? She's just writing an article on me for 'Inside Paper'.

HE POINTS AT HER COPY OF *INSIDE PAPER*.

<u>BRENT:</u> (shouting to room)
Ben, are you wondering who that is? Well, I'll tell you all … If you're wondering who this stranger is wandering around, she's writing an article on me for 'Inside Paper'.

NO-ONE IS INTERESTED.

AN EMPLOYEE WALKS IN.

<u>BRENT:</u>
Where've you been?

<u>EMPLOYEE:</u>
Warehouse.

BRENT:
Well, you've missed me telling everyone … She's writing an article on me. For –
(POINTING AT HIMSELF)
– subject matter.

HE LEADS HER TOWARDS HIS OFFICE.

SCENE 6. INT. BRENT'S OFFICE. DAY.

BRENT AND HELENA ARE SITTING DOWN IN HIS OFFICE.

BRENT:
Right. What do you want to know?

HELENA:
Do you mind if I talk to some of your staff later?

BRENT: (worried)
Why?

HELENA:
Well, my train doesn't leave 'til one-thirty, so I'll hang about if that's okay and have a chat with some of them …

BRENT:
Well, I want to see what they say before –

HELENA:
I'm not going to put anything nasty in.

BRENT:
Well, they won't say anything nasty, so …

HELENA:
Okay.

SHE OPENS HER NOTEBOOK.

<u>HELENA:</u>
Right, so would you like to tell me about your individual outlook on management?

<u>BRENT:</u>
Sure. Put: "David Brent is refreshingly laid-back for a man with such responsibility … "

<u>HELENA:</u>
Yeah, can you just answer in your own words and I'll work it up later.

<u>BRENT:</u>
Yeah.

BRENT THINKS LONG AND HARD ABOUT THIS.

<u>BRENT:</u>
"Brent mused and then replied … "

<u>HELENA:</u>
Sorry, no, David, could you just say what's on your mind and I'm getting it down, so I'll …

<u>BRENT:</u>
Well, are you getting it down, because you're not doing short-hand, and I'm going to be pretty –

HE SNAPS HIS FINGERS.

<u>HELENA:</u>
Just –

<u>BRENT:</u>
Well, okay, your question I suppose was: "Is it difficult to remain authoritative and yet so popular?"

<u>HELENA:</u>
Well, no, that wasn't my question.

BRENT:
Well, shall I answer that one first?

HELENA:
Sorry, no, can we just stick to my questions?

BRENT: (curt)
Well, maybe you should be clear what the question is 'cos I'm getting a little bit ... And that's, you know ...

HELENA:
Okay.

SHE GLANCES DESPAIRINGLY AT THE CAMERA CREW.

SCENE 7. INT. OPEN-PLAN OFFICE. DAY.

DAWN IS LEANING ON TIM'S DESK. THEY ARE LAUGHING AND CHATTING ABOUT SOMETHING. RACHEL JOINS THEM, GATECRASHING THEIR LITTLE TETE-A-TETE.

RACHEL:
What's so funny?

TIM:
Nothing, nothing.

RACHEL:
I was just talking to Emma about ... What is that pub we went to on Friday?

TIM:
Oh, the Jolly Farmer.

GARETH'S PHONE RINGS. HE PUTS IT ON SPEAKER-PHONE.

GARETH:
Gareth Keenan. Hello.

ANGE: (on speaker-phone)
Hi baby. It's Ange.

GARETH:
Alright?

ANGE:
Are you coming around tonight?

GARETH:
I can't. I'm going up Chasers with the lads.

ANGE:
Oh, come round first. We'll have a bit of time together.

GARETH:
Alright.

ANGE:
Have some fun.

GARETH:
Yep. Okay.

ANGE:
Are you going to bring the toys again?

GARETH, EMBARRASSED, GRABS THE RECEIVER, SNAPPING IT OFF SPEAKER MODE.

GARETH: (into receiver)
Erm, yeah … Okay … Yeah … Look forward to … doing it to you too. Alright, bye.

HE HANGS UP. TIM CAN'T BELIEVE HIS LUCK.

TIM:
The toys?

GARETH:
Shut up.

TIM:
What are the toys? Is it Buckaroo?
(LIKE IT'S A SERIOUS QUESTION)
It's not Boggle is it?

GARETH:
Shut up.

TIM:
If it's Kerplunk I'm coming round.

GARETH:
It was actually a private phone call, so –

TIM:
Well, don't put it on speaker-phone then Gareth.

PAUSE.

TIM:
Yeah, the Jolly Farmer ... Is it Hungry Hippos?

RACHEL, TIM AND DAWN LAUGH.

SCENE 8. INT. BRENT'S OFFICE. DAY.

HELENA IS STILL INTERVIEWING BRENT.

HELENA:
Private life, then, just to flesh out David Brent "the man". Is there a better half?

BRENT:
David quipped, "Why buy a book when you can join a library?"

HELENA:
So you play the field?

BRENT:
Well, I'm not going round, like, using chicks 'n' shit, but I'm just, you know, chilling out while I'm young I suppose.

<u>HELENA:</u>
And is there a "chick" in tow at the moment?

<u>BRENT:</u>
Oh, I don't kiss and tell.

<u>HELENA:</u>
I'm just trying to find out if you're in a relationship at the moment.

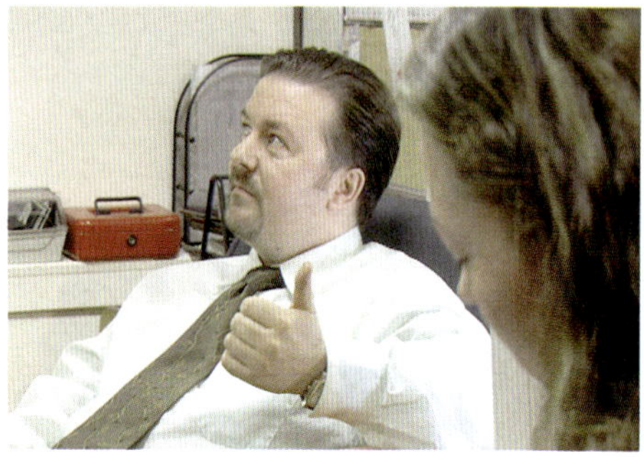

<u>BRENT:</u>
Brent says, "No comment".

<u>HELENA:</u>
Right. So you don't have a girlfriend?

<u>BRENT:</u>
Well, you know, what is a "girlfriend"?

<u>HELENA:</u>
I don't know, someone you'd have sex with?

<u>BRENT:</u> (angry)
Alright, don't get coarse – in a magazine for the public. I don't think you'd win a Pulitzer for filth.

<u>SCENE 9. INT. OPEN-PLAN OFFICE. DAY.</u>

GARETH HAS BOUGHT A BIRTHDAY GIFT FOR HIS FRIEND: AN UGLY, ANIMATED PUPPET CALLED 'DIRTY BERTIE'.

<u>GARETH:</u>
I've got this for my mate, Gobbler. It's his birthday. We're all going up Chasers tonight. Watch this.

GARETH CLAPS HIS HANDS TO DEMONSTRATE 'DIRTY BERTIE'. THE PUPPET WOLF-WHISTLES THEN STARTS SHOUTING AND MAKING THRUSTING MOTIONS.

PUPPET:
Oh yeah, oh yeah! Come on, come on baby! Come on, come on baby!

GARETH:
Watch ... Watch ...

THE PUPPET PLAYS THE 'WILLIAM TELL' OVERTURE AND ITS UNDERPANTS START TO VIBRATE.

PUPPET:
Oh, oh, oh, oh no!

GARETH: (to TIM)
Watch this. You know Gobbler, don't you? You seen this?

TIM LOOKS UNIMPRESSED. GARETH IS TICKLED PINK. HE CLAPS HIS HANDS TO START THE PUPPET AGAIN.

PUPPET:
Oh yeah, oh yeah! Come on, come on baby! Come on, come on baby!

GARETH:
Watch, watch, watch, watch ... He's gonna love that.
(POINTING)
He comes in his pants!

GARETH, IN FITS, STARTS THE PUPPET YET AGAIN. TIM TOSSES HIS PEN OVER HIS SHOULDER IN FRUSTRATION AND EXITS.

TIM TALKING HEAD. INT. DAY.

TIM:
You know, I don't give myself a hard time about things particularly. Thirty is young now anyway. I'm not someone who has specific goals about, you know, having done this or that by my age: "I should've done this, why haven't I taken that chance?" I just think, well, if you look at life like rolling a dice then my situation now, as it stands, yeah, it may only be a three. If I jack that in now, go for something bigger and better, yep, I could easily roll a six, no problem. I could roll a six; I could also roll a one, okay? So I think sometimes just leave the dice alone.

SCENE 10. INT. OPEN-PLAN OFFICE/RECEPTION. DAY.

GENERAL OFFICE SHOTS. DAWN IS LOOKING PENSIVELY AT TIM WHO ALSO SEEMS TO BE DEEP IN THOUGHT.

SCENE 11. INT. BRENT'S OFFICE. DAY.

BRENT IS STILL CHATTING WITH HELENA.

BRENT:
That's why my professionalism is probably only as important as –
(KNOCK AT THE DOOR)
– come in – my erm, humanism.

DAWN ENTERS THE OFFICE WITH AN ENVELOPE IN HER HAND.

DAWN:
Hi. I just wondered if you've got any time for a little chat?

BRENT:
I've always got time for my staff, Dawn. You know that.
(POINTING THIS OUT TO HELENA)
"He's always got time for his staff."

DAWN:
Before you go –

BRENT: (to HELENA, afterthought)
"Even though a lot happening and his mind should be on other stuff, he still … "
(TO DAWN)
Shoot.

DAWN:
Okay. Before you leave I wanted to hand in my notice.

SHE HANDS THE LETTER TO BRENT.

BRENT:
Oh no. I thought this would happen. Who else is thinking of doing this, Dawn?

DAWN:
I don't think anyone is.

BRENT HANDS THE LETTER BACK TO DAWN.

BRENT:
Don't throw your career away just because I'm leaving, yeah? I know it won't be the same, but you'll probably get to know someone else and –

DAWN:
That's not why I'm actually going.

BRENT:
I've read between the lines, so ...

DAWN: (handing the letter back to BRENT)
Well, you haven't read it.

BRENT: (handing the letter back to DAWN)
Very flattering, but is it just a coincidence that you're handing in your notice when I'm leaving?

DAWN: (handing the letter back to BRENT)
Yes, it is.

BRENT:
Is it?

HELENA:
May I ask, why are you leaving, if you don't mind my asking?

DAWN:
No. I'm gonna go away with my fiancé.

HELENA:
Oh. Where are you going?

DAWN:
The States. Just, er, travelling.

BRENT: (agitated)
Well, alright, okay … We're just …
Yeah, thanks.
(TO HELENA)
What are you gonna write about this because I thought we … ?
(TO DAWN, DISMISSIVELY)
Okay, cheers –
(TO HELENA)
I thought we were … Getting back to … strings to Brent's bow.
A: philanthropist …

SCENE 12. INT. RECEPTION SEATING AREA. DAY

TIM IS SITTING LOST IN THOUGHT. NEIL APPROACHES HIM.

NEIL:
Hiya. Have you got a minute?

TIM:
Yeah, sure.

NEIL SITS DOWN.

NEIL:
I don't know if you know, but when David goes, we're probably going to do an external appointment. But we wondered if you'd do us a favour in the meantime and be caretaker manager for a while.

TIM:
Oh blimey. God.

NEIL:
Just doing David's job for a bit, overseeing, and obviously there'd be acting-up pay.

TIM:
Right, well, that's really flattering, thank you, but listen – I am going to say no, and –

NEIL:
I mean, it's a bit more work for a lot more money.

TIM:
Yeah, I understand. I've got nothing to spend it on so …

NEIL:
It's only temporary.

TIM:
I thought that about this job and I've been here for …

NEIL:
Okay.

TIM:
So I'm … you know. Listen, I think you should give it to Gareth, seriously, I do think you should. He takes things seriously, he's conscientious, he works hard …

OFF-SCREEN WE HEAR 'DIRTY BERTIE' CHANTING.

TIM:
… He's responsible, he knows this place inside out, you know. I think, genuinely, I think he might be the man for it.

OFF-SCREEN, BERTIE'S THEME TUNE KICKS IN.

NEIL:
Great. Thanks Tim, listen – I just wanted to ask.

TIM:
Thank you. Much appreciated. Thank you.

SCENE 13. INT. SMOKERS' ROOM. DAY

TIM, DAWN, GARETH, LEE, OLIVER, MOUSEY SHEILA AND TRUDY ARE SITTING IN THE SMOKERS' ROOM. TIM IS READING OUT SOMETHING FROM A MAGAZINE.

TIM:
It says here that for women, the most important qualities in a man are: eyes, smile, flat stomach –

GARETH: (nodding in agreement)
Yeah.

TIM:
– buttocks.

GARETH:
Yep.

TIM:
You've got good buttocks, Gareth?

GARETH:
Yes.

TIM:
Can we see them?

GARETH:
No. Gay.

TIM:
Okay. Well, let's put it out. Sheila, what do you look for in a bloke?

PAUSE.

SHEILA:
I like blacks.

SILENCE.

NOBODY KNOWS WHAT TO SAY.

OLIVER, WHO IS SITTING NEXT TO SHEILA, UNDERSTANDABLY LOOKS A LITTLE UNCOMFORTABLE.

TIM: (breaking the silence)
Cool. Trudy, what about you?

TRUDY:
I quite like shy men actually.

DAWN:
Yeah, I understand that.

TIM:
Would that bc yours as well?

DAWN:
No.

TIM:
What do you look for in a man?

DAWN:
Rugged good looks.

LEE:
You always told me it was a good sense of humour.

DAWN: (to LEE, trying to keep TIM out of her eyeline)
Yeah, you've got that … You've got a good sense of humour.

LEE:
Yeah, I know. I know.

DAWN TRIES HARD NOT TO LOOK IN TIM'S DIRECTION.

WE SEE TIM'S REACTION.

SCENE 14. INT. OPEN-PLAN OFFICE. DAY.

OFFICE SHOTS. TIM IS SITTING AT HIS DESK, GAZING AT DAWN, WHO IS AT THE PHOTOCOPIER. TIM LOOKS UNHAPPY. HE HAS OBVIOUSLY COME TO SOME DECISION.

SCENE 15. INT. KITCHEN. DAY.

TIM FINDS RACHEL IN THE KITCHEN.

TIM:
Hi Rach, have you got a sec? Can I have a word?

RACHEL:
Mmm …

THEY WALK OVER TO A QUIET AREA OF THE OFFICE.

TIM:
I just wanted to tell you and I don't know how to say it. Oh, this is so hard.

SCENE 16. INT. OPEN-PLAN OFFICE. DAY.

RACHEL IS SITTING AT HER DESK, TEARFUL, BEING COMFORTED BY A COLLEAGUE. GARETH IS WATCHING HER.

GARETH: (to TIM)
Well done. She's crying.

TIM:
I know. Just leave it.

GARETH:
I suppose it's up to me to clear up your mess.

TIM:
Gareth, okay, I'm begging you. Just stay out of it, mate.

GARETH:
No, you dumped her, so it's nothing to do with you any more. She obviously needs something to cheer her up.

HE PICKS UP 'DIRTY BERTIE'. TIM GRABS HIS ARM.

TIM:
Okay. Don't take Dirty Bertie, alright? Don't … don't go at all. I beg you, don't take Bertie.

GARETH:
Overruled.

TIM:
Gareth, if you have to go, okay, don't take Bertie.

GARETH PUTS 'BERTIE' BACK DOWN AND WALKS OVER TO RACHEL.

GARETH:
Hi, I, er –

RACHEL:
Fuck off.

HE WALKS AWAY, ONLY TURNING BACK TO ADD:

GARETH:
Potty mouth.

SCENE 17. INT. RECEPTION SEATING AREA. DAY.

BRENT IS HANDING OUT BUSINESS CARDS AGAIN. HE FINDS A FEMALE EMPLOYEE ON A TEA BREAK.

BRENT: (to EMPLOYEE)
Oh. There you go. So, stay in touch.

EMPLOYEE:
Yeah. Cheers.

SHE TAKES THE CARD. BRENT, FEELING PATERNAL, PATS HER ON THE HEAD.

BRENT TALKING HEAD. INT. DAY.

BRENT:

People can't believe I'm this happy to be leaving and it's not 'cos there's anything wrong with it; it's because, you know I did that thing at the community centre? Well, as I was giving that motivational speech, I could literally see them all getting all motivated from it. And that's, you know ... It's like being born again and it showed me how much I had to offer other people.

SCENE 18. INT. BRENT'S OFFICE. DAY.

BRENT WALKS INTO HIS OFFICE WITH JUDE AND RAY FROM THE MANAGEMENT CONSULTANCY FIRM. HE INTRODUCES THEM TO HELENA.

BRENT: (to HELENA)
And these are the guys from Cooper and Webb, the Management Training Consultants I'm dealing with at the moment. This is Ray, this is Jude.

RAY:
Hi.

BRENT:
This is Helena, she's writing quite a big article on me for 'Inside Paper' – the trade magazine. So, you know, I've mentioned our thing, so ... You don't mind if she sits in on this gig do you?

RAY:
No, not if you don't.

BRENT:
No, I'm coolio. Okay.

SCENE 19. INT. RECEPTION. DAY.

DAWN ANSWERS THE PHONE AT RECEPTION. BEHIND HER, WE SEE GORDON THE MAINTENANCE MAN COME OUT OF THE FIRE DOOR CARRYING A BAG OF TOILET ROLLS. AS EVER, HE'S STUNNED BY THE CAMERA, TRAPPED IN ITS GAZE LIKE A RABBIT IN HEADLIGHTS.

NEIL AND GARETH COME OUT OF THE MEETING ROOM. THEY'RE FINISHING A CONVERSATION.

NEIL:
I'm gonna be in in a few days.

GARETH:
Okay.

NEIL:
Obviously if you've got any problems give me a call at, er …

NEIL IS DISTRACTED BY GORDON, WHO IS STILL PARALYSED BY THE CAMERA.

NEIL:
Erm, see you later. Bye.

NEIL WALKS OUT PAST RECEPTION. GARETH WALKS OVER TO TIM.

GARETH:
Alright, mate?

TIM:
Alright.

GARETH:
Probably wondering who they're gonna offer David's job to. Me.

TIM:
You got it?

GARETH:
Yes.

TIM:
Ah, brilliant. Congratulations.

GARETH:
Thank you. Things are going to start changing round here soon. You can start bucking your ideas up, starting with your appearance.

TIM CANNOT BELIEVE THE MONSTER HE'S CREATED.

GARETH:
It's going to be a well-oiled tight ship round these here parts.

SCENE 20. INT. BRENT'S OFFICE. DAY.

BRENT CONTINUES HIS CONVERSATION WITH RAY AND JUDE. HELENA IS STILL PRESENT.

HELENA:
So, what sort of management training is it?

RAY:
We, we specialise in –

BRENT: (interrupting)
Well, I'll tell her. They use celebrity speakers –
(POINTS TO HIMSELF)
– expert speakers, and my personal tip is my rise to the top, which gives it a whole new edge, so ... Okay, so ... Where are we? Shoot.

RAY:
Um, we'd like to thank you very much for the time you've given us –

BRENT:
No sweat. It's what I do.

RAY:
– but we won't be using you again, I'm afraid.

BRENT IS SHELL-SHOCKED.

BRENT:
You won't be? Why not?

RAY:
It's just not exactly what we were looking for.

BRENT:
No, I know but I'll do it how you …
I did it like that 'cos that was the vibe of the day, wasn't it? And I'll just, you know, but I'll do it differently. How do you, how do you want me to do it?

RAY:
We have a very specific idea of what it is that we're looking for and we know –

BRENT: (utterly broken)
Oh, fuckin' hell.

AWKWARD PAUSE.

JUDE:
We would like to say thank you.

BRENT: (dismissive)
Yeah, yeah, yeah, yeah, yeah. Yaddah yaddah yaddah. Go on then, get ...
Timewasters, again.

JUDE:
We're really sorry about –

BRENT:
Oh, get out. Go on. Thank you. Wasting my time.

SILENTLY AND SLOWLY RAY AND JUDE GATHER THEIR STUFF AND EDGE OUT OF THE DOOR, LEAVING HELENA ALONE WITH BRENT. HE LOOKS AT HER.

HELENA:
Oh, you mean me as well?

BRENT:
Yeah.

SHE GATHERS HER THINGS TOGETHER.

HELENA:
Would you mind if I just took a quick photo?

BRENT:
No.

SHE FISHES HER CAMERA OUT OF HER BAG. THIS PROLONGS AN ALREADY AWKWARD MOMENT.

SHE TAKES AIM – BUT THERE'S A HOLD-UP.

HELENA:
I'm just waiting for the flash to … The green light … Okay …

EVER THE PROFESSIONAL, BRENT NODS AND STRIKES A POSE.

HELENA TAKES THE PHOTO.

BRENT:
Right.

HELENA:
Can I just take one more for safety?

SHE WINDS THE CAMERA ON. THE PROCESS REPEATS ITSELF. THEY RESUME THE SAME PAINFULLY SILENT POSES AGAIN.

HELENA:
I'm just waiting for the green light.

BRENT:
Yeah. I know.

THE SILENCE IS TORTUOUS. FINALLY HELENA TAKES THE PHOTO.

BRENT:
Right.

SHE MAKES A NOISY EXIT, LEAVING BRENT ALONE, LOOKING DEVASTATED.

SCENE 21. INT. SMOKERS' ROOM. DAY.

DAWN IS SITTING READING A MAGAZINE. TIM JOINS HER.

TIM:
Hello.

DAWN:
Hello.

TIM:
You alright?

DAWN:
Yeah. You?

TIM:
Fine. Uh, am I fine? I've just heard you were leaving.

DAWN:
Blimey.

TIM:
Say it isn't so.

DAWN:
That got around fast.

TIM:
It is … It's true?

DAWN:
Yeah, yeah.

TIM:
Were you going to tell me or – ?

DAWN:
God. Yeah.

TIM:
Right. You were?

DAWN:
Yes.

TIM:
Okay, okay … You're going to another job?

DAWN:
No, um, Lee and I are going to go away.

TIM:
On holiday?

DAWN:
No, no. We're going to Florida for about six months. Something like that.

TIM: (shocked)
Six months?

DAWN:
Uhuh. Lee's sister she lives out there and so we could live with her and, er, he's not happy in his job; I'm not happy in mine –

TIM:
So what do you call ... ? Is there a name for this?

DAWN:
I dunno.

TIM:
... whatever you're doing.

DAWN:
Starting again.

TIM:
Right. Starting again?

DAWN:
We're just gonna get our heads together I think and, you know –

TIM:
Um. Cool.

LEE WALKS IN.

TIM:
Oh God, hello. The adventurer. Here he is. She was just telling me about the American thing.

LEE:
Yeah, yeah. My sister's over there, yeah.

TIM:
Brilliant.

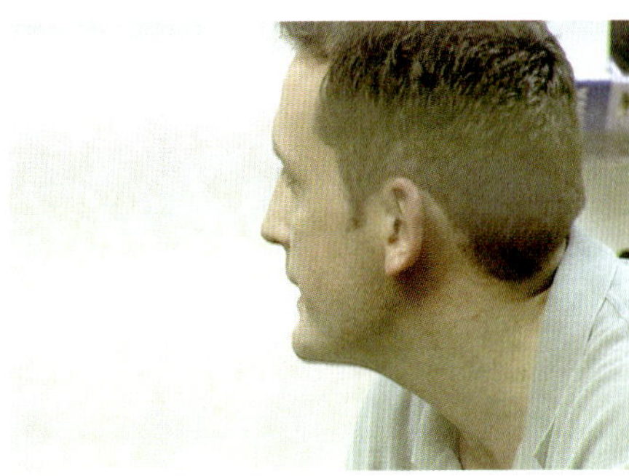

LEE: (to DAWN)
Got a big house, haven't they?

DAWN:
We haven't seen it yet.

LEE:
Seen pictures though; it's a big place.
Her husband's raking it in as well, so...

TIM:
Great.

LEE:
Yeah, we thought we'd get one of them mobile homes, you know, drive up the coast, do the beaches, until the cash runs out. Then I suppose come home or better still get a place out there if we like it. Accommodation's well cheap.

TIM LOOKS PAINED BUT IS TRYING TO MAINTAIN A BRAVE FACE.

TIM:
Is it?

LEE:
And if Dawn gets a job on reception out there, she'll be twice as well off, so it makes sense.

DAWN SOAKS IN THIS HAPPY PROSPECT.

TIM:
Oh, I fancy that. That'd be nice wouldn't it? Brilliant. Well, good luck. I'd better get back to it. Well done, mate.

LEE:
Cheers.

TIM:
Have a great time.

LEE:
Yeah. Looking forward to it.

TIM:
Alright.

LEE: (to DAWN)
Alright, love? Hello, how you doing?

DAWN:
Good.

LEE:
What's that? You looking for swimming costumes or something? Bikinis?

DAWN'S TALKING HEAD BEGINS OVER THIS.

DAWN TALKING HEAD. INT. DAY.

DAWN:
A real relationship isn't like a fairy-tale. If you think that for the next forty years every time you see each other you're gonna glow, or, you know, every time you hold hands there's gonna be electricity, then you're kidding yourself, really. What about reliability, or someone paying the mortgage, or someone who's never been out of work? Those are the more important practical things, you know, in reality.

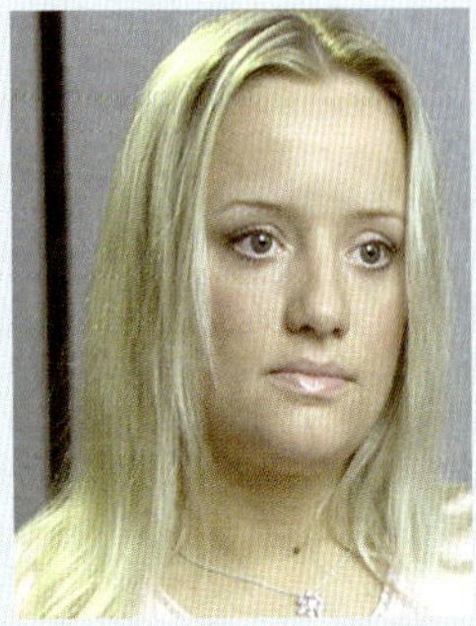

SCENE 22. INT. OPEN-PLAN OFFICE/BRENT'S OFFICE. DAY.

OFFICE SCENES. WE SEE SHEILA LOOK OVER AT OLIVER, QUIET LONGING IN HER EYES.

BRENT IS ALONE IN HIS OFFICE. HE STANDS UP AND BUMPS HIS KNEE ON THE DESK. HE HOBBLES AWAY IN PAIN, THEN WITHOUT WARNING TURNS AND ATTACKS THE DESK VIOLENTLY WITH HIS FOOT.

CUT TO: DAWN WALKING PAST TIM. AS SHE DOES SO SHE FLICKS THE BACK OF HIS NECK. HE SMILES AND THEN LOSES HIMSELF IN THOUGHT.

TIM'S TALKING HEAD BEGINS OVER THIS.

TIM TALKING HEAD. INT. DAY.

TIM:
You know, as I said at the time, when I asked Dawn out, I didn't "ask her out"; I asked her out as a friend, you know. I felt sorry for her because she was having trouble with Lee at the time and it was … No, it wasn't like a, you know – under different circumstances, then sure, something may have happened – but she's going away now, you can't act … You can't change circumstances, you know …

HE TRAILS OFF AND FALLS SILENT FOR A MOMENT.

TIM:
Sorry, excuse me …

TIM SUDDENLY GETS UP AND WALKS OUT OF THE FRAME.

THE CAMERA BEGINS TO MOVE – IT'S OBVIOUSLY BEING LIFTED OFF ITS TRIPOD. THE CAMERAMAN HASTILY FOLLOWS TIM, WHO IS STRIDING PURPOSEFULLY DOWN A CORRIDOR. HE APPROACHES DAWN AT RECEPTION.

TIM:
Dawn, Dawn, can I just have a word in here?

HE LEADS HER INTO THE MEETING ROOM AND CLOSES THE DOOR. THE CAMERA WATCHES THEM THROUGH THE WINDOW.

TIM UNHOOKS HIS INTERVIEW MICROPHONE AND THE SOUND FROM INSIDE THE MEETING ROOM DISAPPEARS.

WE SEE TIM SAYING SOMETHING TO DAWN. WE CANNOT HEAR WHAT IS BEING SAID. DAWN PUTS HER ARMS ROUND HIM AND HUGS HIM, THEN SAYS SOMETHING IN RESPONSE.

PAUSE.

THEY BOTH EMERGE FROM THE MEETING ROOM BUT WE CANNOT READ THEIR FACES.

TIM WALKS PAST THE CAMERA AND WE FOLLOW HIM TO HIS DESK. HE REALISES THAT HE HASN'T GOT HIS MICROPHONE ON. HE CLIPS IT BACK ON AND LIFTS THE MIC TO HIS MOUTH.

TIM:
She said no, by the way.

WE HOLD ON TIM, BACK BEHIND HIS DESK.

SCENE 23. INT. BRENT'S OFFICE. DAY.

NEIL AND JENNIFER ARE SETTLING DOWN WITH BRENT. BRENT IS ACTING DEFIANTLY IN THE FACE OF ADVERSITY. HE IS ALMOST DIGNIFIED.

NEIL:
You alright, David?

BRENT:
Yeah. Fine. You?

NEIL:
Yeah.

BRENT:
Good. Small talk done. Go on.

NEIL:
Okay, thanks very much. Everyone really appreciates what you've done.

BRENT:
Do you?

NEIL:
Okay. Down to business.

NEIL PASSES A PIECE OF PAPER ACROSS TO BRENT. BRENT READS IT.

NEIL:
That's what we've come up with as a redundancy offer.

BRENT:
Yeah. More than I expected.

NEIL:
We've been quite generous.

BRENT:
Bada-bing.

NEIL:
Now, you can leave on the third with your holiday I understand, which is a Tuesday. Now, we wondered if you wanted to come back for a party on the Friday or leave on the Friday before?

BRENT:
Whatever.

NEIL:
Okay. Well, again, thanks very much David.

NEIL OFFERS HIS HAND. BRENT TAKES IT – BUT HOLDS ON.

BRENT:
Don't make me redundant … Please.

NEIL: (embarrassed)
Look, David ...

BRENT: (handing the offer back)
I don't … I've changed my mind. I don't want redundancy. I don't want that. I haven't signed anything so …

NEIL:
Well, David, unfortunately it's not really up to you. I'm sorry.

BRENT, FOR THE FIRST TIME, REALISES HE CAN'T ACT TOUGH HERE.

BRENT: (desperate)
No, okay then … Alright then. Well, I'm asking, okay? Please don't make me redundant.
(TO JENNIFER)
You can, you can talk to someone, Jenny.

JENNIFER:
The wheels are already in motion.

BRENT:
No, well, stop them because –

NEIL:
David, we're not going to discuss this now.

BRENT IS ALMOST IN TEARS.

BRENT:
No, but just say that it's not definite now before you go. And we can … I will try twice as hard, I really will. I know I've been complacent and I'll turn this place around if we just say that it's not definite now, and then we can, um … "You're not going until … " Starting from now. Starting from now.

SILENCE. NEIL AND JENNIFER DO NOT KNOW WHAT TO SAY.

WE HOLD ON THE THREE OF THEM UNTIL WE CAN BEAR IT NO LONGER.

SCENE 24. INT. OPEN-PLAN OFFICE. DAY.

VARIOUS OFFICE SHOTS.

WE SEE BOTH DAWN AND TIM, EACH ALONE AND EACH LOOKING UTTERLY SHELL-SHOCKED.

BRENT'S TALKING HEAD BEGINS OVER THIS.

BRENT TALKING HEAD. INT. DAY.

BRENT:
Life is just a series of peaks and troughs, yeah? And you don't know whether you're in a trough until you're climbing out, or on a peak until you're coming down. And that's it, you know. You never know what's round the corner. But it's all good. Here you are: "If you want the rainbow, you've got to put up with the rain." Do you know which "philosopher" said that? Dolly Parton.
(PAUSE)
And people say she's just a big pair of tits.

CLOSING MUSIC AND END CREDITS, THEN:

WE SEE DAWN BEHIND THE RECEPTION DESK, LOOKING SHAKEN. THE PHONE RINGS AND SHE ANSWERS IT.

DAWN:
Hello, Wernham Hogg …